E S T A T E   P U B L I

CW00674826

CHICHESTER · BOGN

BOSHAM · EAST & WEST WITTERING · MIDI

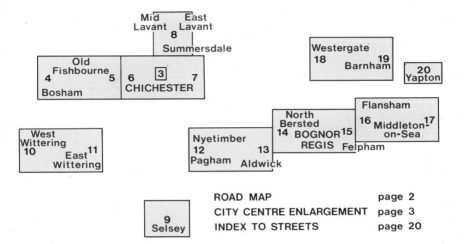

Mid Lavant   East Lavant
8
Summersdale

Old Fishbourne
4   **5**   **6**   **3**   **7**
Bosham   CHICHESTER

Westergate
18   **19**
Barnham
20
Yapton

Flansham
North Bersted
14 BOGNOR **15**   **16** Middleton-**17**
REGIS   Felpham   on-Sea

West Wittering
10   East **11**
Wittering

Nyetimber
12   **13**
Pagham   Aldwick

9
Selsey

Every effort has been made to verify the accuracy of information in this book but the publishers cannot accept responsibility for expense or loss caused by any error or omission. Information that will be of assistance to the user of the maps will be welcomed.

The representation of a road, track or footpath on the maps in this atlas is no evidence of the existence of a right of way.

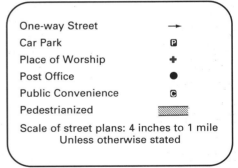

One-way Street   →
Car Park   🅿
Place of Worship   ✚
Post Office   ●
Public Convenience   🅒
Pedestrianized   ▨▨▨

Scale of street plans: 4 inches to 1 mile
Unless otherwise stated

Street plans prepared and published by ESTATE PUBLICATIONS, Bridewell House, TENTERDEN, KENT, and based upon the ORDNANCE SURVEY mapping with the permission of The Controller of H. M. Stationery Office.

The publishers acknowledge the co-operation of the local authorities of towns represented in this atlas.

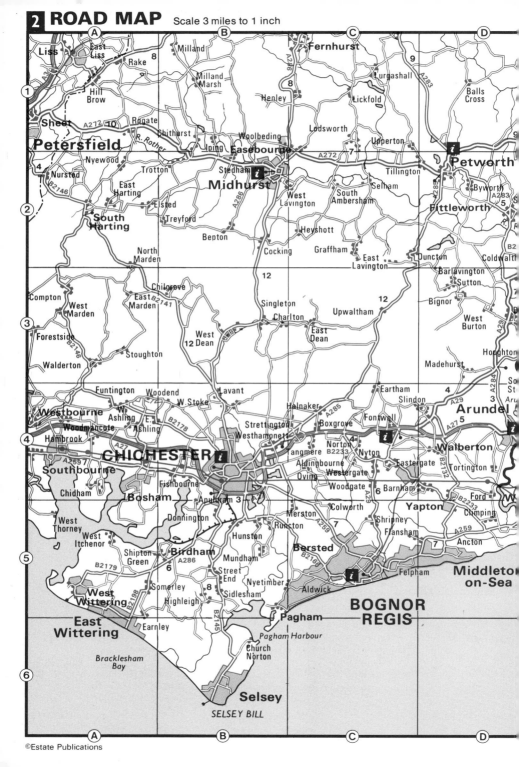

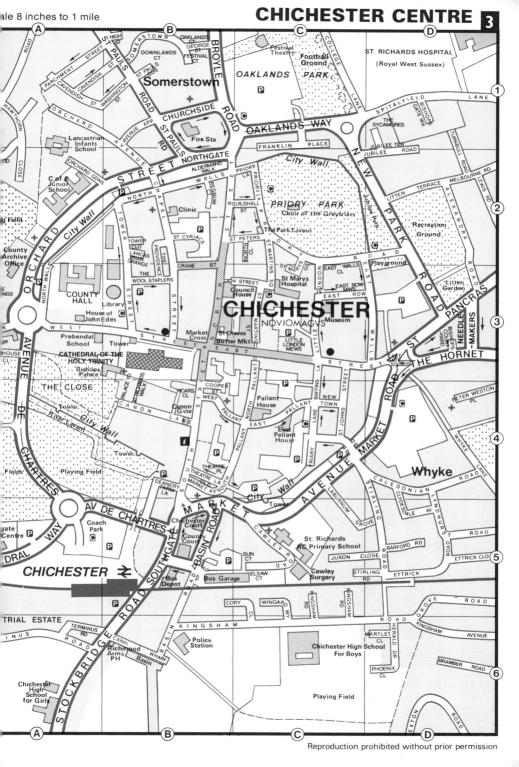

Somerstown

OAKLANDS

Festival Theatre

Football Ground

ST. RICHARDS HOSPITAL
(Royal West Sussex)

OAKLANDS PARK

OAKLANDS WAY

FRANKLIN PLACE

City Wall

PRIORY PARK

Choir of the Greyfriars

The Park Tavern

Lancastrian Infants School

C of E Junior School

County Archive Office

COUNTY HALL

Library

House of John Edes

Prebendal School

Tower

CATHEDRAL OF THE HOLY TRINITY

Bishops Palace

THE CLOSE

River Lavant

City Wall

Tower

Playing Field

Clinic

St Cyriacs

THE PROVIDENCE

LANCAS GRANGE

THE WOOL STAPLERS

CRANE ST

St Peters

St Martins

St Marys Hospital

Council House

Market Cross

St Olaves

Butter Mkt

CHICHESTER

NOVIOMAGVS

Museum

LITTLE LONDON MEWS

St Richards Walk

Vicars Cl

Canon Gate

Canon Lane

Pallant House

East Pallant House

THEATRE PL

i

Recreation Ground

Litten Garden

Playground

EAST WALLS CL

EAST ROW MWS

EAST ROW

EAST GATE SQ

THE HORNET

PETER WESTON PL

COOPER ST

Pallant

Baffins La

New Town

St Johns

Friary

Whyke

CALEDONIAN

STIRLING GROVE

LABURNUM

CLOVESDALE AV

LYNDHURST

ROAD

CHICHESTER ≷

AV DE CHARTRES

Coach Park

Chichester Court

County Court

SUN CT

ELSAW CT

Bus Depot

Bus Garage

St. Richards RC Primary School

Cawley Surgery

JUXON CLOSE

STIRLING RD

ETTRICK

BARFORD RD

ETTRICK CLO

Police Station

Richmond Arms PH

Basin

CORY CL

WINGARD WY

KINGSHAM RD

KINGSHAM

KINGSHAM

Chichester High School for Boys

MARTLET CL

PHOENIX CL

BRAMBER ROAD

KINGSHAM AVENUE

HERALD DR

Chichester High School for Girls

TRIAL ESTATE

TERMINUS RD

CANAL

WHARF

Playing Field

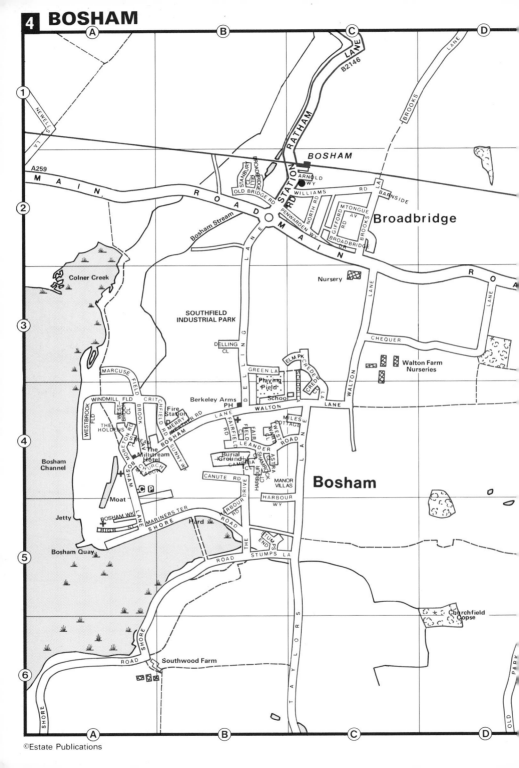

4 BOSHAM

©Estate Publications

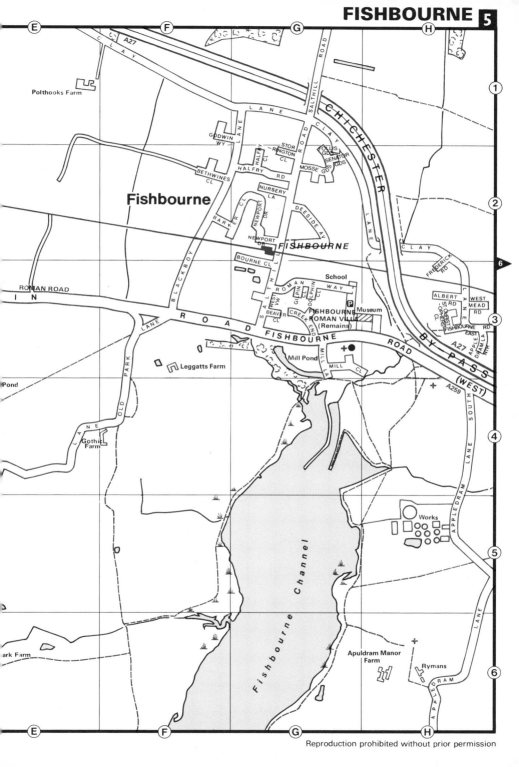

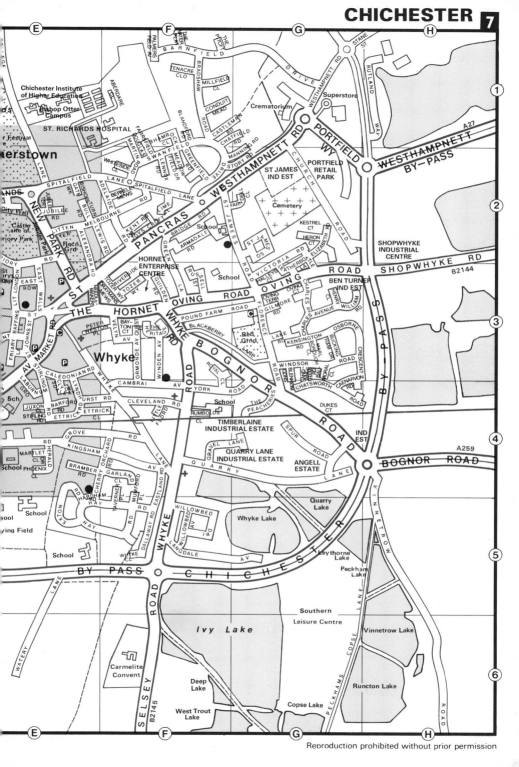

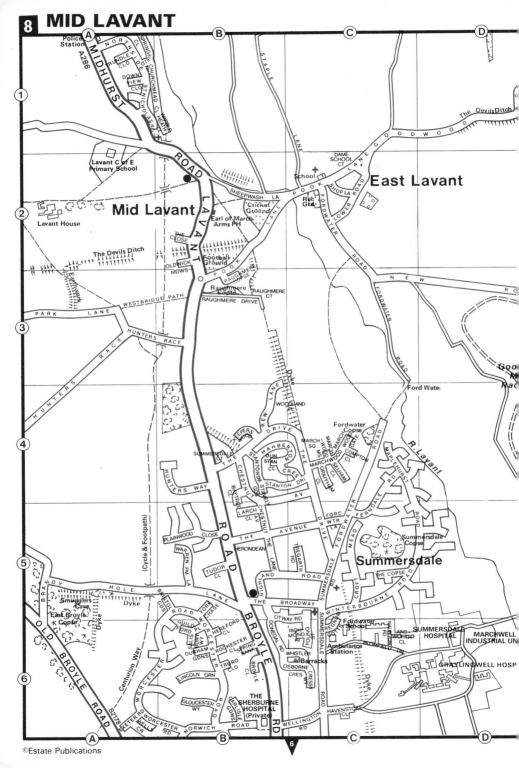

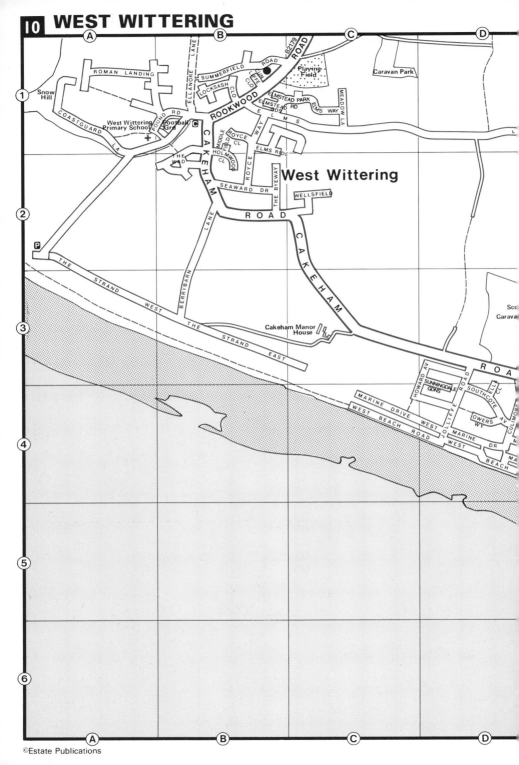

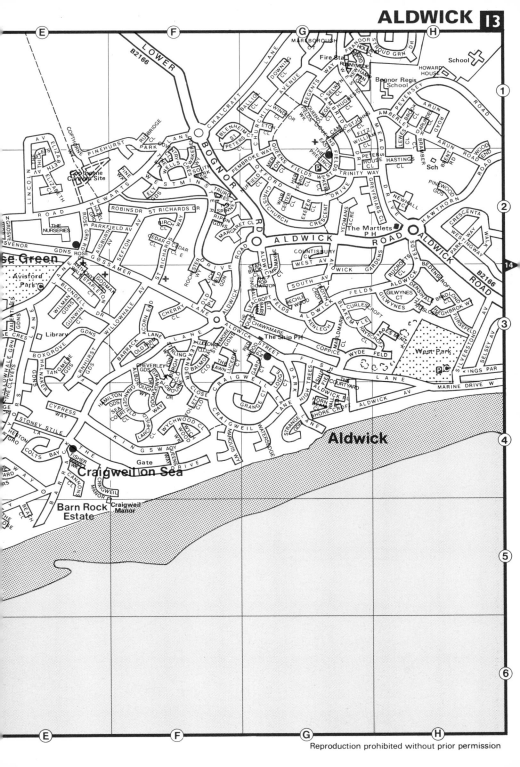

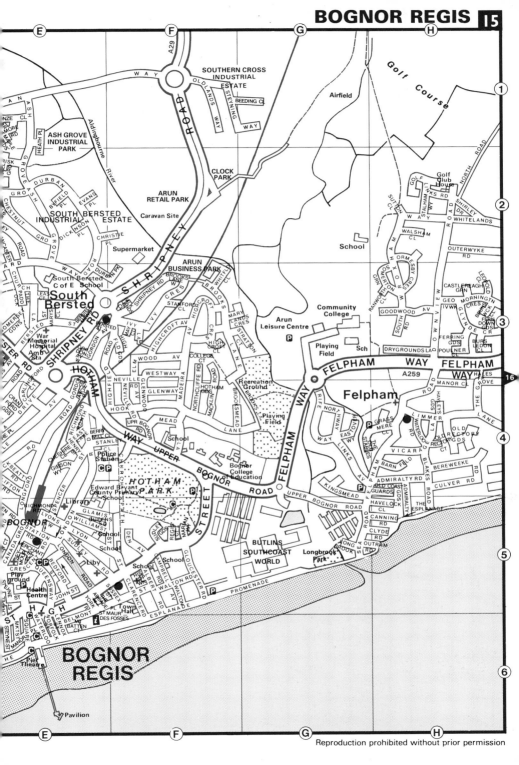

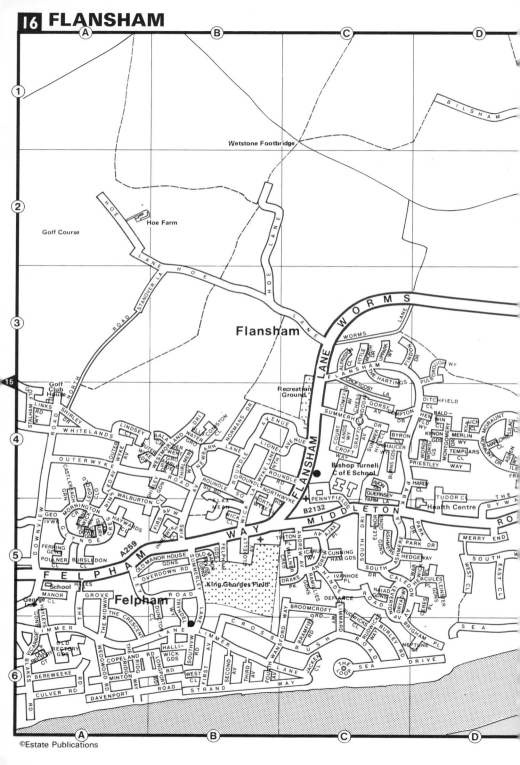

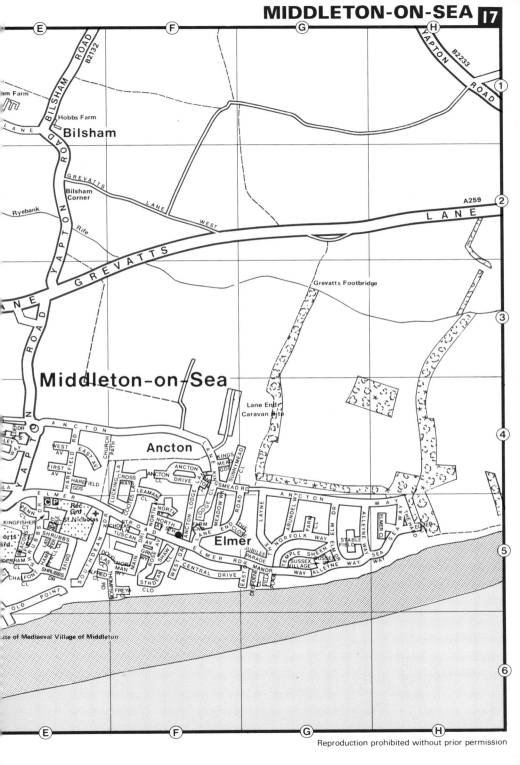

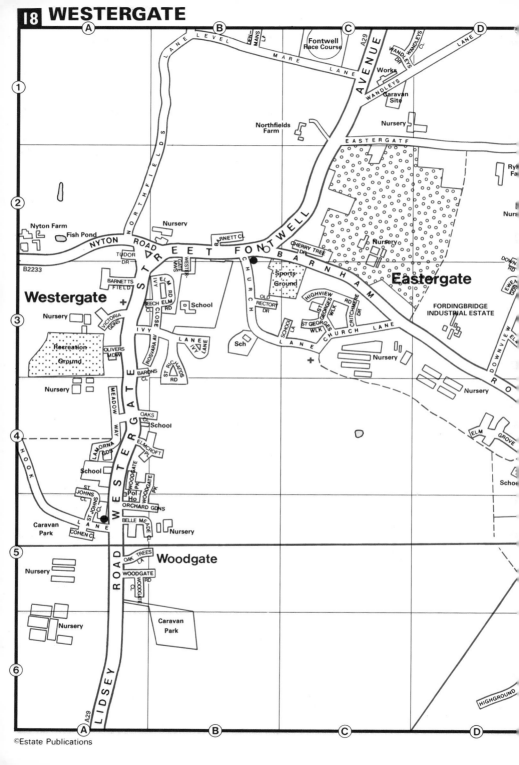

A B C D

1

LANE LEVEL
DEN MANS LA
Fontwell Race Course
A29
WANDLEYS DR
WANDLEYS CL
LANE
MARE LANE
AVENUE
Works
WANDLEYS
Caravan Site

2

Northfields Farm
Nursery
EASTERGATE
NYTON FARM
Fish Pond
NORTHFIELDS
Nursery
B2233
BARNETT CL
CHERRY TREE
Nursery
Ryl Fa
Nurs

FONTWELL
BARNHAM
Eastergate
DOWN RD

TUDOR DR
WESTER- CLANS MNS
Sports Ground
OLD RECTORY DR
HIGHVIEW DR
FORDINGBRIDGE INDUSTRIAL ESTATE
EWE GDS

3

Westergate
BARNETTS FIELD
Nursery
VICTORIA GDNS
STREET
AXE ELM RD
BEECH CL
ELM RD
School
ST GEORGES WLK
CRITCHMERE
DOWNVIEW LA
Recreation Ground
OLIVERS MDW
IVY
ROSWARRAN
LANE
AV
CHURCH
SCHOOL LA
ST GEORGES WLK
CHURCH LANE
Nursery
RO
Nursery
BARONS CL
ST R HATTS RD
Sch
Nursery

4

MEADOW WAY
OAKS CL
School
D
ELM GROVE
HOOK
LAMORNA RDS
ELMCROFT
Schoo
School
WESTERGATE
WOODGATE PK
WOODGATE
WOODGATE PK
Pol Ho
ORCHARD GDNS
ST JOHNS CL
ST JOHNS CL
BELLE M
Nursery
Caravan Park
COHEN CL
LANE

5

OAK TREES LA
Woodgate
Nursery
WOODGATE RD
ROAD
WOODGN
Nursery
Caravan Park

6

LIDSEY
A29
HIGHGROUND

A B C D

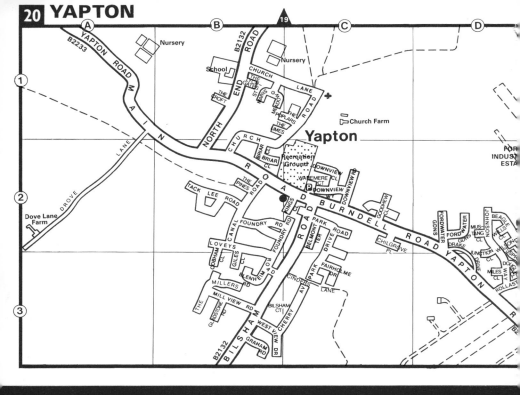

A - Z INDEX TO STREETS
with Postcodes

The Index includes some names for which there is insufficient space on the maps. These names are preceded by an * and are followed by the nearest adjoining thoroughfare.

BOGNOR REGIS

A Beckets Av. PO21   12 D4
Abbottsbury. PO21   12 C5
Acorn End. PO21   13 F3
Addison Way. PO22   14 D1
Admiralty Gdns. PO22   15 H4
Admiralty Rd. PO22   15 H4
Aigburth Av. PO21   13 E2
Ajax Pl. PO22   16 C5
Albert Rd. PO21   15 F5
Alborough Way. PO21   13 F3
Aldbourne Dri. PO21   13 F4
Alder Way. PO22   17 E4
Aldwick Av. PO21   14 B6
Aldwick Felds. PO21   14 A5
Aldwick Gdns. PO21   14 B5
*Aldwick Grange,
  Craigwell La. PO21   14 A6
Aldwick Pl. PO21   14 B6
Aldwick Rd. PO21   14 A5
Aldwick St. PO21   14 A6
Alexander Clo. PO21   13 F3
*Alexandra Ter,
  Clarence Rd. PO21   15 F5
Alfred Clo. PO22   17 E5
Alfriston Clo. PO22   16 C3
Alleyne Way. PO22   17 G5

Alperton Clo. PO21   12 D4
Amberley Dri. PO21   14 B4
Ambleside Clo. PO22   16 B4
Ancton Clo. PO22   17 F4
Ancton Dri. PO22   17 F4
Ancton La. PO22   17 E4
Ancton Lodge La. PO22   17 F5
Ancton Way. PO22   17 G4
Andrew Av. PO22   16 C5
Annadale Av. PO21   15 E4
Anson Rd. PO21   12 D3
Apple Gro. PO21   12 D4
*Argyle Circus,
  Argyle Rd. PO21   15 E5
Argyle Rd. PO21   15 E5
Arnhem Rd. PO21   14 D3
Arun Rd. PO21   14 B4
Arundel Clo. PO21   14 B4
Arundel Way. PO21   17 G5
Ash Gro. PO22   15 E1
Ashcroft Way. PO21   12 C6
Ashmere Gdns. PO22   16 C5
Ashmere La. PO21   16 C5
Ashurst Clo. PO21   14 B2
Aspen Way. PO22   16 D4
*Aston Ct,
  Lyon St. PO21   15 E5
*Avisford Ter,
  Parkfield Av. PO21   13 E2
Avon Clo. PO22   16 C4

Bala Cres. PO22   16 B4
Baldwin Clo. PO22   16 D4
Balliol Clo. PO21   14 A4
Balmoral Clo. PO21   13 F3
Bank View Clo. PO22   15 E4
Barn Feld. PO22   15 H4

Barons Mead. PO21   12 C5
Barrack La. PO21   13 E4
Barton Clo. PO21   12 C4
Barton Rd. PO22   14 C1
Bassett Rd. PO21   14 D5
Bay Ct. PO21   12 D5
Bay Walk. PO21   12 D5
Beach Clo. PO21   13 E5
Beach Rd. PO21   12 B6
Beaconsfield Clo. PO22   17 E5
Beatty Rd. PO21   15 E4
Bedenscroft. PO21   14 B5
Bedford Av. PO21   14 B2
Bedford St. PO21   15 E5
Beeding Clo. PO22   15 G1
Bell Ct. PO21   13 E3
Belmont St. PO21   15 E6
*Benizi Ct,
  Hislop Wk. PO21   15 F5
Bereweeke Rd. PO22   15 H4
Berghstede Rd. PO22   14 D2
*Berkeley Ct,
  The Esplanade. PO21   15 F5
Berry La. PO22   14 C1
Berry Mill Clo. PO21   15 E5
Bersted Green Ct. PO22   14 D2
Bersted Mews. PO22   15 E3
Bersted St. PO21   15 E3
Bickleys Ct. PO21   14 B3
Bilsham La. PO22   16 D1
Bilsham Rd. PO22   17 E1
Binsted Av. PO21   16 A5
Birch Clo. PO21   13 F2
Birdham Clo. PO21   14 B3
Bishops Clo. PO21   12 C5
Blakemyle. PO21   13 G3
Blakes Rd. PO22   15 H4
Blenheim Ct. PO21   14 A4

Blondell Dri. PO21   13 E3
Boleyn Dri. PO21   12 D4
Bowley La. PO21   12 B1
Bowling Green Clo.
  PO21   12 D4
Boxgrove Gdns. PO21   13 E3
Bradlond Clo. PO21   14 C5
Braemar Way. PO21   14 B1
Bramber Clo. PO21   14 B4
Bramfield Rd. PO22   16 C6
Bramley Gdns.PO22   14 D1
Brazwick Av. PO21   14 B1
Brent Rd. PO21   14 C4
Brickfield Clo. PO21   14 D3
Bridorley Clo. PO21   12 D3
Brigham Pl. PO22   16 C6
Bronze Clo. PO22   15 E1
Brook Clo. PO21   14 B4
Brooklands. PO21   12 C4
Brooks La. PO21   15 F3
Brooks La West. PO21   15 F3
Brooksmead. PO22   15 F4
Broomcroft Rd. PO22   16 C5
Brunswick Clo. PO21   15 H3
Buckland Dri. PO21   12 D3
Bucknor Clo. PO21   12 D3
Bucksham Av. PO21   14 B1
Burchett Walk. PO21   14 B3
Burley Rd. PO22   16 C6
Burngreave Ct. PO21   14 C5
Burnham Av. PO21   14 D5
Burnham Gdns. PO21   14 D5
Burns Gdns. PO21   16 C4
Bursledon Clo. PO22   16 A5
Byfield Pl. PO22   15 E2
Byron Clo. PO21   16 C4

Caledon Av. PO22   16 C5

Cambridge Dri. PO21   14
Cambridge Walk. PO21   14
Campbell Rd. PO21   15
Canada Gro. PO21   15
Canning Rd. PO22   15
Cannons Clo. PO21   13
Canterbury Co. PO21   15
Cardinals Dri. PO21   12
Carlingford Ct. PO21   15
Carlton Av. PO21   12
Carousel Ct. PO22   14
Castlereagh Grn. PO22   16
Cavendish Rd. PO21   14
Cedar Clo. PO21   13
Cedar Clo East. PO21   13
Central Av. PO21   14
Central Dri. PO22   17
Central Dri. PO21   14
Ceres Pl. PO22   16
Chalcraft La. PO21   14
Chalfont Clo. PO22   17
Channel Vw. PO21   12
Charlwood St. PO21   14
Charnwood Rd. PO22   14
Chaucer Way. PO22   16
Chawkmare Coppice.
  PO21   14
Cherry Clo. PO21   13
Cheshire Clo. PO21   14
Chesswood Av. PO22   15
Chestnut Gro. PO22   15
Cheverley Gdns. PO21   15
Chichester Rd. PO21   14
Chipley Ct. PO21   14
Christchurch Cres. PO21   14
Christie Pl. PO22   15
Church Clo. PO21   12

ch La. PO21 12 A6
ch La. PO22 15 E3
ch Path PO22 17 E4
ch Path. PO21 15 F4
ch Way. PO21 12 C4
chill Av. PO21 14 A4
chill Walk. PO21 12 B6
emont Ct,
gh St. PO21 15 F5
ence Gate,
ance Rd. PO21 15 F5
n Rd. PO21 15 E4
sk Wk,
gh St. PO21 15 E5
elly Av. PO22 16 B5
e Rd. PO22 15 H5
sdale Gdns. PO22 14 C1
stguard Par,
arrack La. PO21 13 E4
ge Clo. PO21 14 B4
ge Clo. PO21 15 F3
er Av. PO21 14 C3
Bay. PO21 13 E4
pton Dri. PO22 16 C4
ston Clo. PO22 16 B4
vay Dri. PO21 12 C6
es La. PO22 17 F5
land Rd. PO22 16 A6
pins Ct,
iddleton Rd. PO22 16 D5
horne Way. PO21 13 E1
ishley Grn. PO22 15 E2
ishley Rd. PO22 14 D2
ge Clo. PO21 12 D3
atisbury Clo. PO21 14 B5
tlands Way. PO22 16 C4
ntry Clo. PO21 13 F2
rweil La. PO21 13 F4
rweil Manor. PO21 13 E4
ford Gdns. PO21 15 E4
cent Rd. PO21 15 E5
centa Walk. PO21 14 C5
s Way. PO22 16 C4
cost La. PO21 16 C3
is Bush Rd. PO22 16 B6
sways. PO21 17 F4
er Rd. PO22 15 H4
ingham Gdns.
22 16 C5
scroft. PO21 13 G3
et Walk. PO22 14 D1
ess Way. PO21 13 E4

La. PO21 14 A6
enport Rd. PO22 16 A6
ds Clo. PO21 16 C5
odene Clo. PO22 17 G5
ance Pl. PO22 16 C5
Av. PO21 15 F5
nam Clo. PO22 17 E5
sihale. PO21 14 B5
vent Gro. PO22 16 B4
onshire Pl. PO21 14 D5
onshire Rd. PO21 14 D5
anson PO. PO22 15 E2
nfield Clo. PO22 16 D4
phin Ct,
Market St. PO21 15 E6
set Rd. PO21 17 E5
glas Clo. PO22 14 C3
e Clo. PO22
vercourt,
airlands. PO21 14 C2
ning Clo. PO21 14 A4
nlands Clo. PO22 12 C3
nview Rd. PO22 15 H3
e Park. PO22 16 C5
Av. PO22 12 D3
ad Way. PO22 16 C5
grounds La. PO22 15 H3
es Meadow. PO21 12 D3
cton Clo. PO22 16 B5
pan Park. PO22 15 E3
ean Rd. PO22 15 E2
nam Clo. PO22 12 C5
ston Dri. PO22 14 D2
riston Par,
Durlston Dri. PO22 14 D2

Av. PO21 17 E4
Clo. PO22 16 D5
st Dean,
shripney Rd. PO22 15 E3
e Dri. PO22 17 G5
e Front PO21 12 C6

East Lake. PO22 15 E4
East Mead. PO21 12 C5
Eastover Way. PO21 15 G4
Edinburgh Clo. PO21 13 F3
Edwen Clo. PO21 12 D2
Elbridge Cres. PO21 13 E4
Eleanor Gdns. PO22 16 C5
Elfin Gro. PO21 14 D5
Elizabeth Av. PO21 13 E1
Elizabeth Clo. PO21 13 E2
*Elizabeth Ct,
Park Rd. PO21 14 D6
Ellasdale Rd. PO21 14 D5
Ellis Way. PO21 12 C5
Elm Clo. PO21 12 C4
*Elm Ct,
Scott St. PO21 14 D6
Elm Dri. PO22 17 G5
Elm Gro. PO21 14 C5
Elmer Clo. PO22 17 H5
Elmer Ct. PO22 17 H5
Elmer Rd. PO22 17 F5
Elmwood Av. PO22 15 F3
Elphin Mews. PO21 14 D5
Ely Gdns. PO21 13 F2
Esher Clo. PO21 12 D3
Essex Rd. PO21 14 D3
Eton Clo. PO21 14 A4
Evans Pl. PO22 15 E2
Exeter Clo. PO21 14 B5

Fairlands. PO21 14 C2
Fairway. PO21 12 D5
Falklands Clo. PO21 15 F3
Faresmead. PO21 14 B6
Farm Clo. PO22 17 G5
Farm Cnr. PO22 17 F5
Felpham Gdns. PO22 16 B5
Felpham Rd. PO22 15 H4
Felpham Way. PO22 15 G4
Ferndown Gdns. PO21 16 A5
Fernhurst Gdns. PO21 13 E3
Ferring Gdns. PO22 16 A5
Finch Gdns. PO21 14 D1
Findon Dri. PO22 16 C3
Firs Av. PO22 16 B5
Firs Av West. PO22 16 B5
First Av,
Felpham. PO22 16 B6
First Av, Middleton-
on-Sea. PO22 17 E4
Fish La. PO21 14 B6
Fishermans Wk. PO21 13 E4
Fittleworth Dri. PO22 16 C3
Fitzwilliam Clo. PO21 14 B4
Flansham La. PO21 16 C4
Flansham Park. PO22 16 C4
Flax Mean. PO21 16 B5
Fletcher Clo. PO21 12 D3
Fletcher Way. PO21 14 D3
Follett Clo. PO21 13 F4
Fourth Av. PO21 16 B6
Frandor Rd. PO21 14 B3
Freya Clo. PO21 17 F5
Friary Clo. PO21 16 D4
Frith Rd. PO21 14 C4
Frobisher Rd. PO21 12 D3
Fursefeld. PO21 14 C6

Gainsboro Rd. PO21 15 E5
Garden Ct. PO21 13 G3
George IV Walk. PO21 15 E5
Gibson Way. PO21 15 E4
Gilwynes. PO21 14 B5
Gilwynes Ct. PO21 14 B5
Glamis St. PO21 15 E5
Glencathra Rd. PO21 14 D5
Glenelg Clo. PO21 14 B2
Glenway. PO22 15 F4
Glenwood Av. PO22 15 F4
Gloster Dri. PO21 12 C4
Gloucester Rd. PO21 15 F5
Glynde Cres. PO21 16 A5
Godman Clo. PO21 13 E3
Golden Acre. PO21 12 C5
Golf Links Rd. PO22 15 H2
Goodwood Av. PO22 15 H3
Gordon Av. PO21 15 E4
Gordon Av West. PO21 15 E4
Gorse Av. PO21 16 C4
Gossamer La. PO21 13 E2
Grafton Clo. PO21 16 C4
Grange Ct. PO21 13 G4
Grangefield Way. PO21 13 F4
Grangewood Dri. PO21 13 F3
Grassmere Clo. PO21 15 H4

*Grassmere Par,
Grassmere Clo. PO22 15 H4
Gravits La. PO21 14 C3
Green Rd. PO21 13 E2
Green Way. PO22 17 F5
Greencourt Dri. PO21 14 B2
Greenlea Av. PO21 12 D3
Greenways. PO21 12 C4
Greenwood Av. PO22 14 D2
Greenwood Clo. PO22 14 D2
Grevatts La. PO22 17 E3
Grevatts Lane West.
PO22 17 E2
Greyfriars Clo. PO21 14 B5
Greynville Clo. PO21 12 D3
Greystone Av. PO21 14 B1
Grosvenor Gdns. PO21 13 E2
Grosvenor Way. PO21 13 E2
Guernsey Farm La.
PO22 16 C4
Gunwin Ct. PO21 13 E3

Hadley Clo. PO22 17 E4
Hales FP. PO22 15 H3
Halliwick Gdns. PO22 16 B6
Halnaker Gdns. PO21 13 E3
Hambledon Pl. PO21 14 D5
Hamilton Gdns. PO21 13 F4
Hampden Clo. PO22 17 E5
Hampshire Av. PO21 14 B5
Hampton Av. PO21 14 B4
Harbour Rd. PO21 12 B6
Harbour View Rd. PO21 12 B5
Hardy Clo. PO22 16 D4
Harefield Gdns. PO22 17 E4
Harefield Rd. PO22 17 E4
*Harfield Ct,
High St. PO21 15 F5
Hatherleigh Clo. PO21 14 C3
Hatherleigh Gdns. PO21 14 C3
Havelock Clo. PO21 15 H5
Havelock Rd. PO21 15 E4
Hawkins Clo. PO21 12 D3
Hawks Pl. PO22 14 D1
Hawthorn Rd. PO21 14 B5
Haydon Clo,
Aldwick. PO21 13 E4
Haydon Clo,
Bognor Regis. PO21 14 D4
Hayleys Gdns. PO22 15 H4
Haywards Clo. PO22 16 A5
Hazel Gro. PO21 13 E2
Hazel Rd. PO22 14 D2
Heath Pl. PO22 15 E1
Hechle Wood. PO21 14 A6
Hedgeway. PO22 16 C5
Heghbrok Way. PO22 14 C6
Henfield Way. PO22 16 D4
Henry St. PO21 15 E4
Hercules Pl. PO22 16 D5
Heron Clo. PO22 14 D1
Heron Mead. PO21 12 B6
Hertford Clo. PO21 14 A4
Heston Gro. PO21 13 E4
Hewarts La. PO21 15 E5
High St. PO21 15 E5
High Trees. PO21 14 B6
Highcroft Av. PO21 15 F3
Highcroft Clo. PO21 15 F3
Highcroft Cres. PO22 15 F3
Highfield Gdns. PO22 15 F3
Highfield Rd. PO22 15 F3
Highgate Dri. PO21 14 B1
Highland Av. PO21 14 D4
Hillsboro Rd. PO21 14 D4
Hinde Rd. PO22 15 F5
Hislop Walk. PO21 15 F5
Hoe La. PO21 16 B3
Holland Clo. PO21 14 B3
Holly Ct. PO21 15 E2
Homefield Av. PO21 16 C4
Homing Gdns. PO22 14 C1
Hook La,
Bognor Regis. PO22 15 F4
Hook La,
Nyetimber. PO21 12 C3
Hook La Clo. PO21 12 C3
Hornbeam Clo. PO21 14 B6
Horns La. PO21 15 F5
Hotham Gdns. PO21 15 F4
Hotham Way. PO21 15 F4
Howard House. PO21 14 C4
Hughes Clo. PO21 14 B4
Hunters Clo. PO21 13 E4

Icarus Way. PO22 16 C5
Ilex Way. PO22 17 E4
INDUSTRIAL ESTATES:
Arun Business. Pk.
PO22 15 F2
Arun Retail Pk. PO22 15 F2
Ash Gro Ind Pk. PO22 15 E1
Clock Pk. PO22 15 F2
South Bersted Ind Est.
PO22 15 E2
Inglewood Clo. PO21 12 D4
Inglewood Dri. PO21 12 D4
Innerwyke Clo. PO22 16 B5
Ivanhoe Pl. PO22 16 C5
Ivy Cres. PO22 15 F3
Ivy La. PO22 15 F3
Ivydale Rd. PO21 14 C4

Jacken Clo. PO21 16 C6
John St. PO21 15 E5
Jubilee Par. PO22 17 G5
June Clo. PO21 13 E2
Juniper Clo. PO22 17 E4

Keats Walk. PO21 14 C5
Keble Clo. PO21 14 B5
Kenilworth Rd. PO21 14 C4
Kenlegh. PO21 13 G3
Kestrel Clo. PO21 12 B6
Kew Gdns. PO21 14 B5
Kilwich Clo. PO22 16 D4
King George Ct. PO21 14 C3
Kingfisher Ct. PO22 17 E5
Kings Dri. PO21 12 C5
Kings Par. PO21 14 C6
Kingsmead. PO21 15 G4
Kingsmead Gdns. PO22 17 F4
Kingsmead Rd. PO22 17 F4
Kingsway. PO21 13 F4
Kynon Gdns. PO21 16 D4
Kyoto Ct. PO21 14 C5

Laburnum Gro. PO22 14 D2
Lagoon Rd. PO22 12 B6
Lake View. PO21 12 C4
Lancaster Pl. PO21 15 E2
Lane End Rd. PO22 17 F5
Langley Clo. PO21 12 D4
Larch Clo. PO22 15 E1
Larchfield Clo. PO21 13 F4
Latiter Clo. PO21 17 E5
Laurel Gro. PO21 15 E2
Lavender Clo. PO22 17 E4
Leaman Clo. PO22 17 F4
Leas Ct. PO21 15 E3
Ledbury Way. PO21 12 C3
Ledra Dri. PO21 12 C5
Leecroft. PO21 14 A6
Leinster Gdns. PO21 16 D5
Lennox St. PO21 15 E6
Leonora Dri. PO21 12 D3
Leopold Clo. PO21 16 A4
Leverton Av. PO21 16 C5
Ley Rd. PO22 16 A5
Lichfield Gdn. PO21 13 F3
Lilac Clo. PO22 16 D4
Limmard Way. PO22 16 C6
Limmer La. PO22 16 A3
Lincoln Av. PO21 13 E2
Linden Ct. PO21 15 E4
Linden Rd. PO21 14 D4
Lindsey Ct. PO22 16 A4
Link Way. PO22 12 C5
Links Av. PO22 15 G4
Lion Rd. PO21 12 C3
Lionel Av. PO22 16 B4
Little Babbsham. PO21 14 A6
Loats La. PO21 14 B1
Lodge Clo. PO22 17 F5
Lodge Ct. PO21 13 G3
Lodsworth Rd. PO21 12 D2
London Rd. PO21 15 E5
Longbrook. PO22 15 G5
Longford Rd. PO21 15 E5
Longport Rd. PO22 16 B6
Lovells Clo. PO22 17 E5
Lower Bognor Rd.
PO21 14 A4
Lucerne Ct. PO21 13 F3
Lucking La. PO22 17 F4
Ludlow Clo. PO21 13 F3
*Lyon Ct,
Lyon St. PO21 15 E5

Lyon St. PO21 15 E5
Lyon St West. PO21 15 E5
Macklin Rd. PO21 15 F4
Madeira Av. PO21 15 F4
Main Dri. PO22 17 F5
Mallard Cres. PO21 12 B6
Malmayne Ct. PO21 14 A5
Malvern Way. PO21 12 C4
Manet Sq. PO21 14 C2
Manor Clo. PO21 15 H4
*Manor Ct,
Manor Way. PO21 17 G5
Manor Park. PO21 15 E6
Manor Pl. PO21 15 E6
Manor Way. PO21 12 D4
Manor Way. PO22 17 G5
Mansfield Rd. PO22 14 D3
Maple Clo. PO22 16 D4
Maple Gdns. PO22 15 E1
Margaret Clo. PO21 14 A5
Marian Way. PO21 15 F5
Marine Dri West. PO21 14 C6
Marine Par. PO21 14 D6
*Marine Pk,
Kings Par. PO21 14 C6
Market St. PO21 15 E6
Markfield. PO22 14 D1
Marlborough Ct. PO21 14 B3
Marlowe Clo. PO22 16 D4
Marquis Way. PO21 13 F4
Marshall Av. PO21 14 D4
Martlet Way. PO21 12 B6
Marylands Cres. PO21 15 F3
Mauldmare Clo. PO21 14 B6
May Clo. PO22 15 F3
Mayfield Clo. PO21 12 D3
Mayfield Rd. PO21 14 C4
Mead La. PO22 15 F4
*Meadow Ct,
Priestley Way. PO22 16 D4
Meadow Walk. PO21 17 F5
Meadow Way. PO21 12 D5
Meadow Way. PO22 14 C2
Merchant St. PO21 15 E5
Merlin Way. PO21 12 B6
Merrion Av. PO22 14 D3
Merry End. PO22 16 D5
Merton Clo. PO21 14 A4
Micklam Clo. PO22 12 D3
Middleton Rd. PO22 16 C5
Mill Park Rd. PO21 12 C3
Minton Rd. PO22 16 A6
Mons Av. PO21 14 D3
Montgomery Dri. PO22 16 D4
Moore Pl. PO21 15 E4
Moorhen Way. PO22 14 D2
Moraunt Dri. PO22 16 D4
Mornington Cres. PO22 16 A5
Mountbatten Ct. PO21 15 E6
Mulberry Ct. PO21 12 B6
Murina Av. PO21 14 D3

Naiad Gdns. PO22 16 C5
Nelson Rd. PO21 14 C5
Neptune Ct. PO22 16 D6
Neville Rd. PO21 15 F4
Newbarn La. PO21 14 B4
Newbarn La. PO21 14 B1
Newhall Clo. PO21 14 B5
Newtown Av. PO21 14 B2
Nightingale Ct. PO21 17 E5
Norbren Av. PO21 14 C3
Norfolk Clo. PO21 14 D6
Norfolk Sq. PO21 14 D6
Norfolk St. PO21 15 E6
Norfolk Way. PO21 17 G5
Norman Way. PO22 17 F5
Normans Dri. PO22 16 B4
Normanton Av. PO21 14 D5
North Av. PO21 17 F5
North Av East. PO22 17 F5
North Av South. PO22 17 F5
North Bersted St. PO22 14 A4
North Rd. PO22 16 A4
Northcliffe Rd. PO22 15 F4
Northcote Rd. PO21 14 C4
Northway. PO22 15 G4
Northwyke Rd. PO22 16 B5
Northwyke Rd. PO22 16 B5
*Norwood Ct,
Wick Lane. 16 B5
Nuffield Clo. PO21 14 A4
Nyetimber Clo. PO22 12 D3
Nyetimber Cres. PO22 12 D3
Nyetimber La. PO21 12 D3

21

Nyetimber Mill. PO21 12 C3
Nyewood Gdns. PO21 14 D5
Nyewood La. PO21 14 C4
Nyewood Pl. PO21 14 D6

Oak Clo. PO22 14 D2
Oak Gro. PO22 15 E2
*Oakland Ct,
　Admiralty Rd. PO22 15 H4
*Oakleigh Ct,
　Aldwick Rd. PO21 14 A6
Oakwood Gdns. PO21 15 E4
Ockley Ct. PO21 15 E5
Ockley Rd. PO21 15 E5
Old Bakery La. PO21 14 D6
Old Coastguards. PO22 15 H4
Old Farm Clo. PO21 13 F3
Old Manor House Gdns.
　PO22 16 A5
Old Pl. PO21 13 F3
Old Point. PO22 17 E5
Old Rectory Ct. PO22 15 H4
Old Rectory Gdns. PO22 15 H4
*Old School Mews,
　Felpham La. PO22 15 H3
Oldlands Way. PO22 15 F1
Olivier Ct. PO21 14 C2
Orchard Way. PO22 15 H2
Ormesby Cres. PO22 15 H2
Osprey Gdns. PO22 14 D1
Outerwyke Av. PO22 16 A4
Outerwyke Gdns. PO22 16 A4
Outerwyke Rd. PO22 16 A4
Outram Rd. PO22 15 G5
Overdown Rd. PO22 16 A5
Oxford Dri. PO21 14 A4
Oxford St. PO21 14 D6

Pagham Rd. PO21 12 B5
Park Dri. PO22 16 D5
Park Rd. PO21 14 D6
Park Ter. PO21 14 D6
Parkfield Av. PO21 13 E2
Parklands Av. PO21 14 D4
Parkway. PO21 14 C5
Payne Clo. PO21 12 C5
*Pebble Clo,
　Macklin Rd. PO22 15 F3
Pembroke Way. PO21 14 A4
Penn Clo. PO22 17 E5
Pennyfields. PO22 16 C5
Peterhouse Clo. PO21 14 B4
Pevensey Rd. PO21 14 B4
Pilgrims Way. PO21 12 D4
Pine Walk. PO21 13 F2
Pinehurst Pk. PO21 13 E1
Pinewood Gdns. PO21 14 C4
Place St Maur des Fosses.
　PO21 15 F5
Plover Clo. PO22 14 D1
Poulner Clo. PO22 16 A5
Priestley Way. PO22 16 D5
*Prince William Ct,
　Lyon St. PO21 15 E5
Princes Croft. PO21 12 C5
Princess Av. PO21 14 C6
Priors Waye. PO21 12 C4
Priory Clo. PO21 12 D5
*Priory Ct,
　Campbell Rd. PO21 15 F5
Promenade. PO21 15 F5
Pryors La. PO21 12 E4
Pulborough Way. PO22 16 D3
Pyrford Clo. PO22 12 D3

Queens Flds Wk. PO21 14 B4
Queens Fields E. PO21 14 B4
Queens Fields W. PO21 14 A4
Queens Mead. PO22 12 B5
Queens Sq. PO21 15 E5
Queensway,
　Bognor Regis. PO21 15 E5
Queensway,
　Craigweil. PO21 13 F4

Radford Rd. PO22 14 D3
Raleigh Rd. PO21 12 D3
Ramillies Gdns. PO22 16 C5
Ranworth Clo. PO22 15 H3
Ravens Way. PO22 14 D1
*Ravenwood Ct,
　Aldwick St. PO21 14 A6
Rayscroft Clo. PO21 13 G3
*Red Ridges,
　Kings Par. PO21 14 C6
Redwood Pl. PO21 13 G3

Regents Way. PO21 14 B4
Regis Av. PO21 12 D5
Regis Ct. PO21 15 F5
Renoir Ct. PO22 14 C2
Renoir Mews. PO22 14 C2
Richmond Av. PO21 14 C5
Richmond Av Way.
　PO21 14 C5
Richmond Rd. PO21 15 E5
Richmond Rd Nth. PO21 15 E4
*Richmond Villas,
　Sea Rd. PO22 15 H5
Rife Way. PO22 15 G4
Ripon Gdns. PO21 13 F2
Robins Dri. PO21 13 F2
Rochester Way. PO21 13 F3
Rock Gdns. PO21 14 D6
Rodney Clo. PO21 13 E2
Romney Broad Wk.
　PO21 14 C2
Rose Av. PO22 17 F5
Rose Ct. PO21 13 F2
Rose Green Rd. PO21 12 D2
Rosemary Clo. PO21 12 D2
Rossalyn Clo. PO21 12 D2
Ross Clo. PO21 12 C3
Roundle Av. PO22 16 B4
Roundle Rd. PO22 16 B4
Roundle Sq. PO22 16 B4
Roundle Sq Rd. PO22 16 B4
Rowan Way. PO21 14 C1
Royal Par. PO21 14 C2
Rucrofts Clo. PO21 14 B5
Rudwicks Clo. PO22 16 C6
Rudwicks Way. PO22 16 C6
Ruislip Gdns. PO21 12 D4
Runnymede Ct. PO21 14 B3
Rusbridge Clo. PO21 13 F1
*Russell Pl,
　High St. PO21 15 F5

Sadler St. PO21 15 E6
St Anthonys Wk. PO21 13 E3
St Clares Gdns. PO21 14 C2
St Johns Clo. PO21 14 B4
St Marys Clo. PO21 15 E3
St Nicholas La. PO22 17 F5
St Peters Clo. PO21 14 A4
St Richards Dri. PO21 13 F2
St Richards Way. PO21 13 F3
*St Thomas Ct,
　St Thomas Dri. PO21 12 B5
St Thomas Dri. PO21 12 B5
St Winifreds Clo. PO21 14 D5
Sandringham Way.
　PO21 14 C4
Sandy Rd. PO21 12 B6
Sandymount Av. PO22 14 D3
Sandymount Clo. PO22 14 D2
Sarisbury Clo. PO22 16 A5
Satinwood Clo. PO22 16 A4
Saxon Clo. PO21 12 B5
Scott Clo. PO21 14 D6
Scott St. PO21 14 D6
Sea Clo. PO22 17 E5
Sea La. PO22 17 E5
Sea La. PO21 14 D6
Sea Rd. PO22 15 G5
Sea Way, Elmer. PO22 17 H5
Sea Way, Middleton-
　on-Sea. PO22 17 D6
Second Av. PO22 12 B5
Seacourt Clo. PO21 13 F4
*Seafield Ter,
　Marine Dri W. PO21 14 D6
*Seaward Ct,
　Chapel St. PO21 15 F5
Second Av. PO22 16 B6
Sefter Rd. PO22 12 C2
Sefton Av. PO21 13 F2
Selsey Av. PO21 14 C6
Selwyn Clo. PO21 14 B4
Servite Clo. PO21 14 D4
Seymour Pl. PO21 14 C5
Shaw Clo. PO22 17 F5
Shearwater Dri. PO22 14 D2
Shelley Rd. PO21 14 D2
Sherwood Clo. PO22 14 C2
Sherwood Rd. PO22 14 C2
Ship Field. PO21 14 B6
Shirley Clo. PO22 14 C2
Shirley Dri. PO22 14 C2
Shirley Gdns. PO22 14 B4
Shorecroft. PO21 14 B6
Shripney Rd. PO22 15 E3

Shrubbs Dri. PO22 17 E5
Silver Birch Dri. PO22 16 D4
Silverdale Clo. PO21 12 C5
Silverston Av. PO21 14 C6
*Simon Ct,
　Crescent Rd. PO21 15 E5
Singleton Clo. PO21 12 D4
Somerset Gdns. PO21 15 E3
Somerton Grn. PO22 15 H3
South Av. PO21 14 B5
South Dri. PO22 16 C5
South Rd. PO22 15 H3
*South Ter,
　Shripney Rd. PO22 15 F3
South Walk. PO21 16 D5
South Way. PO21 14 C3
Southdean Clo. PO22 17 F5
Southdean Dri. PO22 17 E5
Southdown Rd. PO21 14 D5
Southover Rd. PO21 15 E5
Southview Rd. PO22 16 B6
Southwark Walk. PO21 13 F2
*Sovereign Ct,
　Campbell Rd. PO21 15 E5
Spencer St. PO21 15 E5
Springfield. PO21 12 C4
Stable Field. PO22 17 G5
Stalham Way. PO22 15 H2
Stanbrok Clo. PO21 14 A5
Stanford Clo. PO22 15 F3
Stanley Clo. PO21 15 E4
Stanmore Gdns. PO21 13 F3
Stanover La. PO22 16 A3
Stapleton Ct. PO21 13 E3
Station Rd. PO21 15 E5
Steyne. PO21 15 E6
Steyne St. PO21 15 E5
Steyning Way. PO22 15 F1
Stirling Way. PO21 13 F3
Stocker Rd. PO21 14 D6
Stoneage Clo. PO22 15 E1
Stonehill Cres. PO21 12 D2
Stoney Stile Clo. PO21 13 E4
Stoney Stile La. PO21 13 E4
Strand Way. PO22 16 B6
Strange Gdn. PO21 13 G4
Stratton Ct. PO22 15 G3
*Streathleigh Ct,
　Kings Par. PO21 14 C6
Streete Ct. PO21 14 D6
Stroud Green Dri. PO21 14 B3
Sturges Rd. PO21 14 D6
Sudbury Clo. PO21 12 D4
Sudley Gdns. PO21 15 F5
Sudley Rd. PO21 15 E5
Summer La. PO21 12 B4
Summerhill Clo. PO22 16 C4
Summerhill Dri. PO22 16 C4
Summerley La. PO22 16 B5
Sun Park Clo. PO21 14 B2
Sundale La. PO22 16 D4
Sunningdale Gdns.
　PO22 14 D1
Sunnymead Clo. PO22 17 F4
Sussex Ct. PO22 17 G5
Sussex Dri. PO21 12 C4
Sussex St. PO21 15 F5
Sussex Village. PO22 17 G5
Sutherland Clo. PO21 14 D5
Sutton Clo. PO21 15 H2
Swan Dene. PO22 12 B6
Swansea Gdns. PO21 14 D6
Sycamore Rd. PO22 15 E1
Sylvan Way. PO21 14 D5
Sylvia Clo. PO21 12 C4

Tabard Gate. PO21 12 D4
Tamarisk Clo. PO21 15 E2
Tangmere Gdns. PO21 13 E3
Templars Clo. PO22 16 D4
Temple Sheen. PO21 17 G5
Tennyson Rd. PO21 14 C5
The Arcade. PO21 15 E5
The Avenue. PO21 14 D5
The Byeway. PO21 12 D5
The Byway. PO22 16 D5
The Causeway. PO21 12 C5
The Clevets. PO21 13 E4
The Close. PO21 13 E5
The Close, Elmer. PO22 17 F5
The Court. PO21 12 C5
The Courtyard. PO21 14 B6
The Crescent. PO21 12 C5
The Crescent. PO22 16 A5
The Croft. PO21 14 B3
The Dell. PO22 14 C2

The Drive. PO21 13 E4
The Dunes. PO21 12 D5
The Esplanade. PO21 15 E6
The Glade. PO21 12 C5
The Green. PO21 12 C5
The Grove. PO22 16 A5
The Hard. PO22 17 H5
The Hartings. PO22 16 C3
The Hollies. PO21 14 B3
The Hopgarton. PO21 14 A5
The Lawn. PO21 13 F3
The Layne. PO22 17 G5
The Loop. PO22 16 C6
*The Maples,
　Hambledon Pl. PO21 14 D5
*The Mews,
　Merchant St. PO21 15 E5
The Midway. PO22 16 A6
The Nurseries. PO21 13 E2
The Nyetimbers. PO21 12 C3
The Orchard. PO21 13 E4
The Orchard Clo. PO21 14 D5
The Paddock. PO21 15 E3
The Parade. PO21 12 B6
The Pound. PO21 14 A6
The Precinct. PO21 14 B4
The Ridgway. PO22 16 A6
The Ridings. PO21 13 E4
The Spinney. PO21 13 F2
The Thickets. PO21 13 E2
The View. PO21 12 C5
*The Willows,
　Victoria Dri. PO21 14 D4
Third Av. PO22 16 B6
Thirlmere Way. PO22 16 B4
Thompson Rd. PO22 17 F5
Thorndene Av. PO21 14 D5
Thrusloes. PO21 14 A5
Tinghall. PO21 14 A5
Tithe Barn Clo. PO21 12 D5
*Tithe Barn Ct,
　Tith Barn Way. PO21 12 D5
Tithe Barn Way. PO21 12 D5
Town Cross Av. PO21 14 D4
*Trafalgar Ct,
　Norfolk Clo. PO21 14 D6
Trendle Grn. PO21 14 B5
Trinity Way. PO21 14 B4
Triton Pl. PO22 16 C5
Trotyn Croft. PO21 13 G3
Truro Cres. PO21 13 F2
Tryndel Way. PO22 16 B5
Tudor Clo. PO22 16 D4
Tuscan Av. PO22 17 F5
Tyne Way. PO21 13 F2

Ullswater Gro. PO22 16 B4
Uppark Way. PO22 16 C3
Upper Bognor Rd. PO21 15 F4

Valentines Gdns. PO21 13 E3
Van Dyke Pl. PO22 14 C2
Van Gogh Pl. PO22 14 C2
Venus La. PO21 12 A6
Vicarage La. PO22 15 H4
*Victoria Ct,
　Aldwick Rd. PO21 14 D6
Victoria Dri. PO21 14 D6
Victoria Rd. PO21 14 D6
Victoria Rd Sth. PO21 14 D6
*Victoria Ter,
　Sea Rd. PO22 15 H5
*Victory Ct,
　Norfolk Clo. PO21 14 D6
Villa Plage. PO22 17 G5
Viscount Dri. PO21 12 C5

Wadhurst Clo. PO21 14 D4
Wakefield Way. PO21 13 F2
Walburton Clo. PO21 16 A4
Wallfield. PO21 14 B6
Wallner Cres. PO22 16 C5
Walsham Clo. PO21 15 H2
Walton Av. PO21 15 F5
Walton Rd. PO21 15 F5
Wansford Way. PO22 16 B6
Warblers Way. PO22 14 D1
Warwick Av. PO22 12 C3
Warwick Pl. PO22 16 D5
Waterloo Rd. PO21 15 H4
Waterloo Sq. PO21 15 E6
Watersedge. PO21 13 G4
Waverley Rd. PO21 14 C6
Webb Clo. PO21 12 C6
Wedgwood Rd. PO21 14 A6
Well Rd. PO21 12 B6

Wellington Rd. PO21
Wells Cres. PO21
Wessex Av. PO21
West Av. PO21
West Av. PO22
West Clo,
　Felpham. PO22
West Clo, Middleton-
　on-Sea. PO22
West Dri. PO22
West Dri. PO21
West Front Rd. PO21
West Meads Dri. PO21
West St. PO21
Westfield. PO22
Westingway. PO21
Westloats Gdns. PO21
Westloats La. PO21
Westminster Dri. PO21
Westmoreland Dri.
　PO22
Westway. PO22
Whitebeam Way. PO22
Whitelands. PO22
Whiteways. PO22
Whiteways Clo. PO22
Whitfield Clo. PO22
Wick Clo. PO22
Wick La. PO22
*Widworthy Mews,
　Sylvan Way. PO22
William St. PO21
Willow Way. PO21
Willowhale Av. PO21
Willowhale Grn. PO21
Wilman Gdns. PO12
Windmill Clo. PO21
Windsor Clo. PO21
Winston Clo. PO21
Winston Cres. PO21
Wolsey Clo. PO21
Wood End. PO21
Wood St. PO21
Woodfield Clo. PO21
Woodlands Rd. PO22
Worcester Clo. PO21
Wordsworth Gdns.
　PO22
Worms La. PO22
Wren Cres. PO22
*Wrenfield Pl,
　Scott Clo. PO21
Wroxham Way. PO21
Wychwood Clo. PO21
Wychwood Walk. PO21
Wyde Feld. PO21
Wyke La Nth. PO22
Wythering Clo. PO21

Yapton Rd. PO22
Yeomans Acre. PO21
Yew Tree Clo. PO22
York Rd. PO21

CHICHESTER

Aberdare Clo. PO19
Adelaide Rd. PO19
Albert Rd. PO19
Aldermans Wk. PO19
Alexandra Rd. PO19
Answorth Clo. PO19
Appledram Lane Nth.
　PO19
Appledram Lane Sth.
　PO20
Armadale Rd. PO19
Arnold Way. PO18
Ashburnham Clo. PO19
Astra Clo. PO18
*Augusta Ct,
　Regnum Cotts. PO19
Avenue App. PO19
Avenue de Chartres.
　PO19

Baffins La. PO19
Balmoral Clo PO19
Barford Rd. PO19
Barker Clo. PO18
Barlow Rd. PO19
Barnfield Dri. PO19
Barnside. PO18
Barton Rd. PO19

Rd. PO19 3 B6
n Ct. PO19 7 F3
ee Clo. PO19 8 B4
er Clo. PO19 5 G3
1 Av. PO20 6 C3
ave Cres. PO19 6 D6
lo. PO19 6 C1
ley Mews. PO19 7 F2
vines Clo. PO18 5 F2
am Rd. PO19 6 B6
p Luffa Clo. PO19 6 B2
p's Courtyard.
19 3 D3
psgate Walk. PO19 3 D1
berry La. PO19 7 F3
boy La. PO19 5 F3
lford Rd. PO19 7 F1
eim Gdns. PO19 7 G4
field Dri. PO19 8 C6
or Rd. P.19 7 F3
am La. PO18 4 B4
am Wk. PO18 4 A5
he Clo. PO19 5 G2
shaw Rd. PO19 7 F1
ber Rd. PO19 3 D6
dy Hole La. PO19 8 A5
Oake Clo. PO19 6 C1
e Rd. PO19 7 F2
l Gdns. PO19 8 B5
dbridge Dri. PO18 4 C2
dbridge Mill. PO18 4 B2
x Av. PO19 4 A4
xs La. PO19 4 C2
e Clo. PO19 8 B6
e Rd. PO19 3 B1
ngham Dri. PO19 7 G3
ter Way. PO19 6 D5

narvon Rd. PO19 7 G4
lonian Rd. PO19 7 F4
orai Av. PO19 7 F4
oria Clo. PO18 4 B4
l Wharf. PO19 3 B6
l Wharf Rd. PO19 6 D4
n La. PO19 3 B4
erbury Clo. PO19 6 D1
te Rd. PO18 4 B4
ton Rd. PO19 6 C1
sle Gdns. PO19 8 B6
sells Rd,
way Rd. PO19 8 B5
eman Rd. PO19 7 F1
edral Mews. PO19 6 D1
edral Way. PO19 3 A5
ndish St. PO19 3 A1
ey Rd. PO19 3 C5
r Dri. PO19 6 C3
dler Rd. PO19 3 B2
el St. PO19 3 B2
es Av. PO19 7 G3
ield Rd. PO19 7 F1
sworth Rd. PO19 7 G4
uer La. PO18 4 C3
y Orchard Rd. PO19 7 E4
nut Av. PO19 8 B4
ester By-Pass.
19 6 A2
ch Meadow. PO18 4 A4
ch Rd. PO. PO19 7 G2
hmead Clo. PO18 8 A1
hside. PO19 3 B1
La. PO19 6 A2
land Rd. PO19 7 F4
on Ct,
arland Clo. PO19 7 F4
sdale Av. PO19 3 D4
ge La. PO19 3 C1
ton Clo. PO19 8 C4
uit Mead. PO19 7 F1
er St. PO19 3 B4
Clo. PO19 3 B5
sells Rd,
way Rd. PO19 8 B5
e St. PO19 3 B3
e Clo. PO19 4 C4
e La. PO18 4 C3
x End. PO19 5 G3
y Way. PO19 8 C6
nfield Rd. PO18 4 A4
Mead. PO19 8 C5
ie Gdns. PO19 6 D6
Clo. PO19 6 C5
eld Clo. PO19 6 C6

way Rd. PO19 7 F5
e School Ct. PO18 8 C2

Deanery Farm La. PO19 3 B4
Deeside Av. PO19 5 G2
Delling Clo. PO18 4 B3
Delling La. PO18 4 B4
*Dempsey Rd,
Otway Rd. PO19 8 C5
Dolphin Clo. PO19 5 G3
Dolphin Mews. PO19 6 B3
Donegal Rd. PO19 8 B6
Donnington Pk. PO19 6 B6
Douglas Martin Rd. PO19 7 F2
Downlands Clo. PO19 3 B1
Downview Clo. PO18 8 A1
Draymans Mews. PO19 7 F3
Dukes Ct. PO19 7 G4
Duncan Rd. PO19 6 C1
Dunstan Clo. PO19 8 B4
Durham Gdns. PO19 8 B6
Durnford Clo. PO19 6 C2

East Pallant. PO19 3 C4
East Row. PO19 3 C3
East Row Mews. PO19 3 C3
East St. PO19 3 B3
East Walls. PO19 3 D3
East Walls Clo. PO19 3 C3
*Eastgate Ct,
Velyn Av. PO19 7 F3
Eastgate Sq. PO19 3 D3
Eastland Rds. PO19 7 F4
Elizabeth Rd. PO19 7 G2
Elm Park. PO18 4 C3
Elsaw Ct. PO19 3 C5
Ettrick Clo. PO19 3 D5
Ettrick Rd. PO19 3 D5
Exeter Rd. PO19 8 A6
Exton Rd. PO19 3 D6

Fairfield Clo. PO18 4 B4
Fairfield Rd. PO18 4 B4
Farrsfield. PO19 7 F1
Ferndale Rd. PO19 8 C5
Festival Ct. PO19 3 B1
Fishbourne Rd. PO19 5 G3
Fishbourne Rd E. PO19 6 A3
Fishbourne Rd W. PO19 6 A3
Flaxman Av. PO19 6 B3
Florence Rd. PO19 7 G3
Follis Gdns. PO19 5 G2
Fordwater La. PO19 8 C5
Fordwater Rd. PO19 8 C2
Forge Clo. PO19 6 C6
Franklin Pl. PO19 3 C1
Frederick Rd. PO19 6 A2
Friary La. PO19 3 C4

Garland Clo. PO19 7 F4
George St. PO19 3 B1
Gifford Rd. PO14 4 C2
Gilbert Rd. PO19 6 C1
Gilmore Rd. PO19 7 G3
Gilpin Clo. PO19 5 G3
Gloucester Way. PO19 8 B6
Godwin Way. PO18 5 F1
Goodwood Rd. PO18 8 C1
Gordon Av. PO19 6 C6
Graffham Clo. PO19 8 C4
Gravel La. PO19 7 F4
Graydon Av. PO19 6 C5
Green La. PO18 4 B3
Green La. PO19 7 F2
Greenfield Rd. PO19 7 F2
Grenville Gdns. PO19 6 C5
Grosvenor Rd. PO19 6 D5
Grove Park. PO19 6 B3
Grove Rd. PO19 3 D4
Guilden Rd. PO19 7 F3
Guildford Pl. PO19 8 B6
Guildhall St. PO19 3 C2

Halfry Clo. PO18 5 G2
Halfry Rd. PO18 5 G2
Halleys Ct. PO19 7 G3
Hannah Sq. PO19 6 B2
Harberton Cres. PO19 8 B4
Harbour Clo. PO18 4 B4
Harbour Rd. PO18 4 B5
Harbour Way. PO18 4 B4
Hardham Rd. PO19 7 E5
Havenstoke Clo. PO18 8 C6
Hawthorn Clo. PO19 8 A1
Hay Rd. PO19 7 E5
Henry Clo. PO19 7 G3
Henty Gdns. PO19 3 A3
Herald Dri. PO19 3 D6
Hereford Clo. PO19 8 B6

Heron Ct. PO18 7 G2
Herondean. PO19 8 B5
High St, Bosham. PO18 4 A5
High St,
Somerstown. PO19 6 D1
Highland Rd. PO19 8 B5
Hilary Rd. PO19 6 C1
Hunters Race. PO19 8 A4
Hunters Way. PO19 8 B4

INDUSTRIAL ESTATES:
Angell Est. PO19 7 G4
Ben Turner Ind Est.
PO19 7 G3
Hornet Enterprise Centre
PO19 7 F3
Marchwell Ind Est.
PO19 8 D6
Portfield Retail Pk.
PO19 7 G2
Quarry La Ind Est.
PO19 7 F4
St James Ind Est. PO19 7 G2
Shopwhyke Ind Centre.
PO19 7 H2
Southfield Ind Pk.
PO18 4 B3
Timberlaine Ind Est.
PO19 7 F4
Woodruff Business
Centre. PO19 6 C4
Infirmary Ter. PO19 6 D1

*Jeffreys Av,
Whistler Av. PO19 8 C6
John Arundel Rd. PO19 6 C2
Joys Croft. PO19 7 F2
Jubilee Rd. PO19 3 D2
Jubilee Ter. PO19 3 D1
Juxon Clo. PO19 3 D5

Keepers Wood. PO19 8 B4
Kensington Rd. PO19 7 G3
Kent Rd. PO19 7 F2
Kestrel Ct. PO19 7 G2
King George Gdns. PO19 6 D1
Kings Av. PO19 6 D5
Kingsham Av. PO19 3 D6
Kingsham Rd. PO19 3 B6

Laburnum Gro. PO19 3 C4
Lake Rd. PO19 7 G3
Lancastrian Grange.
PO19 3 B2
Langdale Av. PO19 7 F5
Langton Rd. PO19 6 B2
Lavant Rd. PO19 8 B2
Larch Clo. PO19 8 B5
Leander Rd. PO18 4 B4
Leatherbottle La. PO19 7 G3
Leigh Rd. PO19 6 C4
Lennox Rd. PO19 7 F2
Lewis Rd. PO20 3 D2
Lime Clo. PO19 7 F2
Lincoln Grn. PO19 8 B6
Lion St. PO19 3 C3
Litten Ter. PO19 3 D2
Little Breach. PO19 6 D1
Little London. PO19 3 C3
Little London Mews.
PO19 3 C3
Littlefield Rd. PO19 7 F4
Lower Rd. PO18 8 C2
Lyndhurst Rd. PO19 3 D4

Main Rd. PO18 4 A2
Manning Rd. PO19 7 F2
Manor Clo. PO19 6 C6
Manor Villas. PO19 4 B4
Maplehurst Rd. PO19 8 C4
Marchwood. PO19 8 C4
Marchwood Gate. PO19 8 C4
Marchwood Mws. PO19 8 C4
Marchwood Sq. PO19 8 C4
Marcuse Field. PO18 4 A3
Marden Av. PO19 6 C6
Mariners Ter. PO19 4 A5
Market Av. PO19 3 B5
Market Rd. PO19 3 C2
Marlborough Clo. PO19 7 G3
Martlet Clo. PO19 3 D6
Meadowfield Dri. PO19 7 F2
Melbourne Rd. PO19 3 D2
Merryweather Rd. PO18 4 B4
Midhurst Rd. PO18 8 A1
Miles Cottage. PO18 4 C4

Mill Clo. PO19 5 G3
Mill La. PO19 5 G3
Millfield Clo. PO19 7 F1
Millwood Ct. PO19 3 A2
Montague Av. PO18 4 C2
Montague Rd. PO19 6 C2
Moreton Rd. PO18 4 A4
Mosse Gdns. PO19 8 A4
Mount La. PO19 3 A3
Mumford Pl. PO19 7 F4

Naunton Rd. PO19 8 C6
Needlemakers. PO19 3 D3
Neville Rd. PO19 6 B2
New Park Rd. PO19 3 C2
New Rd. PO19 8 C3
New Town. PO19 3 C4
Newells La. PO18 4 A1
Newlands La. PO19 6 B1
Newport Dri. PO19 5 G2
North Clo. PO19 3 C2
North Pallant. PO19 3 C4
North Rd. PO18 4 C2
North St. PO19 3 B3
North Walls. PO19 3 B2
Northgate. PO19 3 B2
Northside. PO18 8 A1
Norwich Rd. PO19 6 C1
Nursery La. PO19 5 G2

Oak Av. PO19 6 C2
Oak Clo. PO19 6 C2
Oaklands Ct. PO19 3 B1
Oaklands Way. PO19 3 C1
Old Bridge Rd. PO18 4 B2
Old Broyle Rd. PO19 8 A6
Old Market Av. PO19 3 B4
Old Park La. PO18 4 D6
Oldwick Mdws. PO18 8 B2
Oliver Whitby Rd. PO19 6 B2
Orchard Av. PO19 3 A1
Orchard Gdns. PO19 3 A2
Orchard St. PO19 3 A3
Ormonde Av. PO19 7 F3
Osborne Cres. PO19 8 B6
Osborne Cres. PO19 7 G3
Otter Clo. PO19 6 C1
Otway Rd. PO19 8 B5
Oving Ct. PO19 7 G3
Oving Rd. PO19 7 F3
Oving Ter. PO19 7 G3

Palace Yd. PO19 3 B4
Palmers Field Av. PO19 7 F1
Parchment St. PO19 3 A1
Park La. PO18 8 A3
Parklands Rd. PO19 3 A1
Peckhams Copse La.
PO20 7 G6
Penwarden Way. PO18 4 B2
Peter Weston Pl. PO19 3 D4
Phoenix Clo. PO19 3 D6
Plainwood Clo. PO19 8 B5
Pook La. PO18 8 B3
Portfield Way. PO19 7 G1
Pound Farm Rd. PO19 7 F3
Poyntz Clo. PO19 6 C6
Priory La. PO19 3 C2
Priory Rd. PO19 3 C2

Quarry La. PO19 7 F4
Queens Av. PO19 6 D5
Queens Gdns. PO19 6 D5
Quest Clo. PO19 7 F3

Ratham La. PO18 4 C1
Raughmere Copse. PO18 8 B3
Raughmere Rd. PO18 8 B3
Raughmere Dri. PO18 8 B3
Regnum Cotts. PO19 8 C6
Regnum Ct. PO19 3 B2
Rew La. PO19 8 B4
Richmond Av. PO19 8 B6
Riverside. PO19 7 F3
Rochester Clo. PO19 8 B6
Roman Way. PO19 5 G3
Royal Clo. PO19 7 F3
Rumbolds Clo. PO19 7 F4
Russell St. PO19 7 F3
Rutland Way. PO19 7 H1

St Bartholomews Clo.
PO19 6 C3
St Christophers Clo.
PO19 6 A3
St Cyriacs. PO19 3 B2

St Georges Dri. PO19 6 C6
St James Sq. PO19 7 G2
St James's Rd. PO19 7 F2
St Johns St. PO19 3 C4
St Martins Sq. PO19 3 C2
St Martins St. PO19 3 C3
St Marys Gdns. PO19 3 C2
St Nicholas Rd. PO19 8 A1
St Pancras. PO19 3 D3
*St Pancras Ct,
St Pancras. PO19 7 F3
St Pauls Gdns. PO19 3 B1
St Pauls Rd. PO19 3 B1
St Peters. PO19 3 C2
St Richards Wk. PO19 3 B4
St Wilfrids Rd. PO19 6 B2
Salisbury Way. PO19 8 B6
Salthill La. PO19 6 A1
Salthill Rd. PO19 5 G3
Sandringham Rd. PO19 7 G3
School La. PO18 4 C3
Selham Clo. PO19 8 C4
Selsey Rd. PO20 7 F6
Selsey Rd. PO19 6 C6
Senator Gdns. PO19 5 G2
Shamrock Clo. PO18 4 B4
Shamrock Clo. PO19 7 F1
Sheepwash La. PO18 8 B2
Sherborne Rd. PO19 6 C3
Sherlock Av. PO19 6 C2
Shop La. PO18 8 C2
Shopwhyke Rd. PO20 7 H3
Shore Rd. PO18 4 A6
Somerstown. PO19 3 B1
South Bank. PO19 6 D5
South Pallant. PO19 3 B4
South St. PO19 3 B4
Southfields Clo. PO19 6 D6
Southgate. PO19 3 B5
Spitalfield La. PO19 3 D1
Springbank. PO19 8 B6
Springfield Clo. PO18 8 A1
Spur Rd. PO19 7 G4
Stanbury Clo. PO19 4 B2
Stane St. PO19 7 G1
Stanton Dri. PO19 8 B4
Staple La. PO18 8 B1
Station Rd. PO18 4 B2
Stavely Gdns. PO19 8 B4
Stirling Rd. PO19 3 D4
Stockbridge Gdns. PO19 6 C6
Stockbridge Rd. PO19 3 A6
Storrington Clo. PO19 5 G2
Story Rd. PO19 7 G2
Stream Clo. PO18 4 A4
Stumps End. PO18 4 B5
Stumps La. PO18 4 B5
Summersdale Ct. PO19 8 B4
Summersdale Rd. PO19 8 C5
Sun Ct. PO19 3 C5
Sunny Way. PO18 4 B4
Swanfield Dri. PO19 7 F2

Taverner Pl. PO19 7 F5
Taylors La. PO18 4 C6
Tenacre Clo. PO19 7 F1
Terminus Rd. PO19 3 A6
The Avenue. PO19 8 B5
The Broadway. PO19 8 B5
The Close. PO18 8 B2
The Copse. PO18 8 C5
The Drive. PO18 4 B5
The Drive. PO19 8 B4
The Heritage. PO19 7 F3
The Holdens. PO19 4 A4
The Hornet. PO19 3 D3
The Lane. PO19 8 B5
The Maltings. PO19 3 A3
The Peacheries. PO19 7 G4
The Pitcroft. PO19 7 F1
The Providence. PO19 3 B2
*The Ridgeway,
Whitby Rd. PO19 6 C2
The Sycamores. PO19 3 D1
The Waterplat. PO19 7 F1
The Woolstaplers. PO19 3 B3
Theatre La. PO19 3 B4
Theatre Pl. PO19 3 B4
Tollhouse Clo. PO19 3 A3
Tower Clo. PO19 3 B2
Tower St. PO19 3 B2
Tozer Way. PO19 7 F3
Tregarth Rd. PO19 8 C5
Trundle Clo. PO19 8 A1
Truro Clo. PO19 8 B6
Tudor Clo. PO19 8 B5

Turnbull Rd. PO19 3 D2
Turnpike Clo. PO19 6 C6

Upton Rd. PO19 6 D5

Velyn Av. PO19 7 F3
Vicars Clo. PO19 3 B4
Victoria Rd. PO19 7 G3
Vinnetrow Rd. PO20 7 H4

Walnut Av. PO19 6 C2
Walton La. PO19 4 B4
Warble Heath Clo. PO18 8 B1
Warren Farm La. PO19 8 B5
Washington St. PO19 3 A1
Waterside Dri. PO19 6 D6
Watery La. PO19 7 E6
Wellington Rd. PO19 8 B6
Wells Cres. PO19 8 A6
West Gate. PO19 6 C3
West Pallant. PO19 3 B4
West St. PO19 3 A3
West View. PO19 5 G3
Westbridge Path. PO18 8 A3
Westbrook Av. PO18 4 A4
Westbrook Field. PO18 4 A4
Westhampnett By-Pass.
    PO19 7 H2
Westhampnett Rd. PO19 7 F2
Westmead Rd. PO19 6 A3
Westward Clo. PO18 4 B4
Whistler Av. PO19 8 B6
Whiteside Clo. PO19 7 F2
Whyke Clo. PO19 7 F5
Whyke La. PO19 3 D4
Whyke Rd. PO19 7 F3
William Rd. PO19 7 G3
Williams Rd. PO18 4 C2
Willow Ct. PO19 6 B3
Willowbed Av. PO19 7 F5
Willowbed Dri. PO19 7 F5
Wilson Clo. PO19 6 B2
Winchester Dri. PO19 6 D1
Winden Av. PO19 7 F3
Windmill Field. PO18 4 A4
Windsor Rd. PO19 7 G3
Wingard Way. PO19 3 C5
Winterbourne Rd. PO19 8 C5
Wiston Av. PO19 6 C5
Woodland Pl. PO19 8 B4
Woodlands La. PO19 6 D1
Worcester Rd. PO19 8 A6

York Chase. PO19 8 B5
York Rd. PO19 7 F4
Young St. PO19 8 C6

EAST WITTERING/ WEST WITTERING

*Admiralty Ct,
    Northern Cres. PO20 11 E4
*Admiralty Row,
    Northern Cres. PO20 11 E4
Armada Ct. PO20 11 G5
Ascot Clo. PO20 11 E3
Avebury Clo. PO20 11 H6
Axford Clo. PO20 11 H5
*Azara Par,
    Bracklesham La. PO20 11 G5
Barn Rd. PO20 11 F4
Barn Walk. PO20 11 E4
Barton Way. PO20 11 G4
Beech Av. PO20 11 G5
Bennetts Clo. PO20 11 E3
Berrybarn La. PO20 10 B3
Bookers La. PO20 11 H3
Bourne Ct. PO20 11 F5
Bracklesham Clo. PO20 11 G5
*Bracklesham Ct,
    Bracklesham La. PO20 11 G5
Bracklesham La. PO20 11 G5
Briar Av. PO20 11 E2
Cakeham Rd. PO20 10 B1
Cakeham Way. PO20 11 E3
Cambridge Av. PO20 11 E3
Charlmead. PO20 11 H3
Church Farm La. PO20 11 F3
Church Rd. PO20 11 E4
Clappers La. PO20 11 G4
Clayton La. PO20 11 G3
Coastguard La. PO20 10 A1
Coney Clo. PO20 11 E4
Coney Rd. PO20 11 E4
Coney Six. PO20 11 E5

Cormorant Way. PO20 11 F5
Culimore Clo. PO20 10 D4
Culimore Rd. PO20 10 D4
Cunliffe Clo. PO20 10 B1
Downview Clo. PO20 11 F4
Earnley Manor Clo.
    PO20 11 H4
Earnley Rd. PO20 11 H4
East Bracklesham Dri.
    PO20 11 G5
Elcombe Clo. PO20 11 H5
Ella Clo. PO20 10 D4
Ellanore La. PO20 10 B1
Elm Clo. PO20 11 G5
Elms La. PO20 10 B1
Elms Ride. PO20 10 B1
Elms Way. PO20 10 C1
Elmstead Gdns. PO20 10 B1
Elmstead Pk Rd. PO20 10 B1
Ely Clo. PO20 11 E3
Eton Dri. PO20 11 E3
Farm Rd. PO20 11 G5
Field Rd. PO20 11 F4
First Av. PO20 11 G6
Fox Warren Clo. PO20 11 E3
Furzefield. PO20 11 E2
Garden Av. PO20 11 G5
Grayswood Av. PO20 11 G5
*Green Ct,
    Northern Cres. PO20 11 E4
Hale Clo. PO20 11 G5
Harmony Dri. PO20 11 G5
Harrow Dri. PO20 11 E3
Haven Ct. PO20 11 E4
Hilton Pk. PO20 11 F3
Holmwood Clo. PO20 10 B1
Howard Av. PO20 10 D3
Joliffe Rd. PO20 10 D4
Kestral Clo. PO20 11 F5
*Kimbridge Pk,
    Kimbridge Rd. PO20 11 F5
Kimbridge Rd. PO20 11 F5
*Kingfisher Par,
    Northern Par. PO20 11 E4
Lacock Clo. PO20 11 H6
Legion Way. PO20 11 F5
Leigh Ct. PO20 11 H6
Locksash Clo. PO20 10 B1
Longlands Rd. PO20 11 E4
Manton Clo. PO20 11 H5
Marine Clo. PO20 10 D4
Marine Dri. PO20 10 D4
Marine Dri West. PO20 10 C4
Marineside. PO20 11 G6
Meadow La. PO20 10 C1
Meadows Rd. PO20 11 F4
Middlefield. PO20 10 B1
Middleton Clo. PO20 11 G5
Mill Gdns. PO20 11 E3
Nab Walk. PO20 11 E5
Nagels Clo. PO20 11 F5
New Par. PO20 11 E4
Northern Cres. PO20 11 E3
Oakfield Av. PO20 11 E4
Oakfield Rd. PO20 11 E4
Old Farm Clo. PO20 11 G5
Owers Way. PO20 10 D4
Oxford Clo. PO20 11 E3
Peerley Clo. PO20 11 F5
Peerley Rd. PO20 11 F5
Piggery Hall La. PO20 11 E2
Plover Clo. PO20 11 G5
Pond Rd. PO20 11 G5
Pound Rd. PO20 10 B1
Roman Landing. PO20 10 A1
Rookwood Rd. PO20 11 E2
Rostock Ct. PO20 11 G5
Royce Clo. PO20 10 B1
Royce Way. PO20 10 D2
Russell Rd. PO20 10 D3
St Annes Ct. PO20 11 E4
Sandpiper Ct. PO20 11 F5
Sandringham Clo. PO20 11 G5
Seafield Clo. PO20 11 F4
Seafield Way. PO20 11 F4
Seafields. PO20 11 G6
Seagate Clo. PO20 10 D4
Seaward Dri. PO20 10 B2
Second Av. PO20 11 G6
Shalbourne Cres. PO20 11 H5
Shingle Walk. PO20 11 E5
Shore Rd. PO18 11 E4
Shoreside Walk. PO20 11 E4
Silver Way. PO20 11 H6
Solent La. PO20 11 E4
Southcote Av. PO20 10 D4

Southdown Ct. PO20 11 F4
Stocks La. PO20 11 E4
Stubcroft La. PO20 11 G4
Summerfield Rd. PO20 10 B1
Sunningdale Gdns.
    PO20 10 D3
Sussex Gro. PO20 11 H6
Tamarisk Walk. PO20 11 E4
The Byeway. PO20 10 B2
The Crescent. PO20 10 D4
The Parade. PO20 11 E4
The Strand East. PO20 10 B2
The Strand West. PO20 10 A2
The Wad. PO20 10 B2
Third Av. PO20 11 G6
Tile Barn La. PO20 11 H1
Tower Pl. PO20 11 E3
Walmsleys Way. PO20 11 H1
Wellsfield. PO20 10 C2
Wessex Av. PO20 11 F4
West Beach. PO20 10 D4
West Beach Rd. PO20 10 C4
West Bracklesham Dri.
    PO20 11 F5
*Westerley Gdns,
    Bracklesham La. PO20 11 G5
Wilton Clo. PO20 11 G5
Windmill Ct. PO20 11 G5
Windsor Dri. PO20 11 E3
Woodborough Clo.
    PO20 11 H5
Wyatt Ct. PO20 11 E4

SELSEY

Acorn Clo. PO20 9 B2
Albion Rd. PO20 9 E3
Allandale Clo. PO20 9 E2
Arnell Av. PO20 9 D3
Barnes Cl. PO20 9 D4
Beach Gdns. PO20 9 C4
Beach Rd. PO20 9 E2
Beacon Dri. PO20 9 D3
Beaufield Clo. PO20 9 C4
Beverley Clo. PO20 9 E3
Birches Clo. PO20 9 B2
Bonnar Clo. PO20 9 C3
Bonnar Rd. PO20 9 C3
Brampton Clo. PO20 9 A2
Bream La. PO20 9 C3
Bridle Way. PO20 9 C3
Broad View. PO20 9 E2
Broadway. PO20 9 B2
Broomfield Rd. PO20 9 E1
Burlington Gdns. PO20 9 D4
Byways. PO20 9 D4
Canadian Cres. PO20 9 D4
Chainbridge La. PO20 9 A1
Chayle Gdns. PO20 9 D3
Cherry Gdns. PO20 9 C4
Chichester Rd. PO20 9 D1
Chichester Way. PO20 9 F1
Church Rd. PO20 9 B3
Clayton Ct. PO20 9 B3
Clayton Rd. PO20 9 B3
Coach House Clo. PO20 9 D2
Colt St. PO20 9 E2
Constable Dri. PO20 9 E2
Coppice La. PO20 9 C2
Cotland Rd. PO20 9 E3
Coxes Rd. PO20 9 C3
Coxswain Way. PO20 9 D4
Crablands. PO20 9 B2
Crablands Clo. PO20 9 C2
Croft Rd. PO20 9 C3
Croft Way. PO20 9 C2
Danefield Rd. PO20 9 B4
Deer Park La. PO20 9 A1
Dennys Clo. PO20 9 D2
Denshare Rd. PO20 9 D1
Domehouse Clo. PO20 9 C1
Drift La. PO20 9 B2
Drift Rd. PO20 9 E1
East Bank. PO20 9 E2
East Beach Rd. PO20 9 E2
East St. PO20 9 D2
East Way. PO20 9 E2
Eels Cross. PO20 9 A1
Elm Gro. PO20 9 C3
Elm Tree Clo. PO20 9 D2
Elmsfield. PO20 9 D2
Fish La. PO20 9 A1
Fishermans Wk. PO20 9 E3
Fontwell Rd. PO20 9 E2

Fraser Clo. PO20 9 E3
Freeways. PO20 9 B1
Gainsborough Dri. PO20 9 D2
Gillway. PO20 9 F1
Glen Cres. PO20 9 D2
Goodwood Ct. PO20 9 D2
Grafton Rd. PO20 9 D4
Granary La. PO20 9 C2
Grant Clo. PO20 9 C2
Green La. PO20 9 C3
Grove Rd. PO20 9 D3
Hanover Clo. PO20 9 E2
Harcourt Way. PO20 9 E1
Heron Clo. PO20 9 A1
Hersee Way. PO20 9 B3
High St. PO20 9 C4
Hillfield Rd. PO20 9 C4
Holford Grn. PO20 9 E2
Horsefield Rd. PO20 9 C2
INDUSTRIAL ESTATES:
    The Londonderry Ind Est.
    PO20 9 C2
Island La. PO20 9 A1
Island Loop. PO20 9 A1
James St. PO20 9 D3
Jones Sq. PO20 9 D4
Kilnwood Clo. PO20 9 E2
Kings Ct. PO20 9 D1
Kingsway. PO20 9 D3
Knap La. PO20 9 C2
Landseer Dri. PO20 9 E2
Langton Clo. PO20 9 C3
Large Acres. PO20 9 C2
Latham Rd. PO20 9 C3
Lawrence Clo. PO20 9 D3
Lewis Rd. PO20 9 C2
Lifeboat Way. PO20 9 D4
Lingfield Way. PO20 9 E2
Littlefield Clo. PO20 9 E2
Lobster La. PO20 9 A1
Longacre. PO20 9 C3
Longacre La. PO20 9 C4
Mackerel La. PO20 9 A1
Magpie La. PO20 9 A1
Malden Way. PO20 9 C2
Malthouse Rd. PO20 9 D2
Manor Farm Clo. PO20 9 D1
Manor Farm Ct. PO20 9 D1
Manor La. PO20 9 E2
Manor Rd. PO20 9 D3
Marine Dri. PO20 9 E2
Marine Gdns. PO20 9 C4
Marisfield Pl. PO20 9 E2
Mcnair Clo. PO20 9 E2
*Mcrae Ct,
    Grant Clo. PO20 9 C2
Meadowland. PO20 9 C3
Medmerry. PO20 9 A2
Merryfield Dri. PO20 9 A2
Mill La. PO20 9 D4
Mixon Clo. PO20 9 D4
Montalan Cres. PO20 9 A2
Mountwood Rd. PO20 9 E1
Murray Rd. PO20 9 C3
Nab Tower La. PO20 9 A1
Netherton Clo. PO20 9 D2
Newfield Rd. PO20 9 F1
North Rd. PO20 9 D2
Northfield. PO20 9 E2
Old Coastguard Cotts.
    PO20 9 A3
Old Farm La. PO20 9 B2
Orchard Av. PO20 9 D3
Orchard Par. PO20 9 E2
Orpen Pl. PO20 9 E2
Otard Clo. PO20 9 D3
Oval La. PO20 9 D4
Pacific Way. PO20 9 D4
Paddock La. PO20 9 E2
Park Av. PO20 9 E2
Park Cres. PO20 9 F1
Park La. PO20 9 F1
Park Rd. PO20 9 F1
Peachey Rd. PO20 9 C3
Pennycord Clo. PO20 9 D4
Prawn Clo. PO20 9 B1
Rife La. PO20 9 A1
Robins Clo. PO20 9 D2
Romney Garth. PO20 9 E2
Round Piece. PO20 9 B1
Roundpiece La. PO20 9 A2
Roundstone Way. PO20 9 E1
Ruskin Clo. PO20 9 E3
Saddle La. PO20 9 C3
St Georges Clo. PO20 9 E1
St Hildas Clo. PO20 9 C3

St Itha Clo. PO20
St Itha Rd. PO20
St Peters Cres. PO20
St Wilfreds Clo,
    East Beach. PO20
St Wilfreds Clo. PO20
Sandy Point. PO20
Sea Gro. PO20
Seagull Clo. PO20
Seal Rd. PO20
Seal Sq. PO20
Seaview Ct. PO20
Sherbourne La. PO20
Slattsfield Clo. PO20
Solent Way. PO20
Southern Rd. PO20
Sparshott Rd. PO20
Spinney Clo. PO20
Sunnymead Clo. PO20
Sunnymead Dri. PO20
The Bridgeway. PO20
The Causeway. PO20
The Close. PO20
The Horseshoe. PO20
The Rookery. PO20
The Wadeway. PO20
The Willows. PO20
Thorny Dri. PO20
Tretawn Gdns. PO20
Turner Way. PO20
Tythe Barn Rd. PO20
Ursula Av. PO20
Ursula Av Nth. PO20
Ursula Sq. PO20
Vincent Rd. PO20
Warner Rd. PO20
Warners La. PO20
Wellington Gdns. PO20
West St. PO20
Western Rd. PO20
Wheatfield Rd. PO20
Widgeon Clo. PO20
Wight Way. PO20
Windsor Rd. PO20
Woodland Rd. PO20
York Rd. PO20

WESTERGATE BARNHAM

Appletree Dri. PO22
Avisford Park Rd. PO22
Bankside. PO22
Barn Rise. PO22
Barnett Clo. PO22
Barnetts Field. PO22
Barnham La. PO22
Barnham Rd. PO22
Barnham Rd. PO22
Barons Clo. PO22
Beech Clo. PO22
Belle Meade Clo. PO22
Birch Clo. BN18
Cherry Tree Dri. PO22
Church La. PO22
Church La. PO22
Cohen Clo. PO22
Copse La. BN18
Critchmere Dri. PO20
Dairy La. BN18
Denmans La. PO22
Dial Clo. PO22
Downview Rd. PO22
Eastergate La. PO20
Elm Gro. PO22
Elm Grove Sth. PO22
Elm Rd. PO22
Elmcroft PO22
Ewens Gdns. PO22
Farnhurst Rd. PO22
Field Clo. BN18
Fontwell Av. PO20
Foxes Croft. PO22
Garden Cres. PO22
Goodacres. PO22
Gospond Rd. PO22
Greenbank. PO22
Halford Dri. PO22
Hedge End Rd. PO22
Henty Clo. BN18
Highground La. PO22
Highview Rd. PO22
Hill La. PO22

PHILIP'S

PENZANCE ST IVES

www.philips-maps.co.uk

First published in 2008 by
Philip's, a division of Octopus Publishing Group Ltd
www.octopusbooks.co.uk
Endeavour House,189 Shaftesbury Avenue
London WC2H 8JY
An Hachette UK Company
www.hachette.co.uk

Second edition 2010, first impression 2010
ISBN 978-1-84907-123-9
© Philip's 2010

Ordnance Survey® This product includes
mapping data licensed
from Ordnance Survey®, with the permission of the
Controller of Her Majesty's Stationery Office.

© Crown copyright 2010. All rights reserved.
Licence number 100011710

Contents

II **Key to map symbols**

III **Key to map pages**

IV **Route planning**

2 **Street maps** at 2¼ inches to 1 mile

14 **Street maps** at 4½ inches to 1 mile

26 **Index**

▼ St Michael's Mount, *J Hughes / Alamy*

Key to map symbols

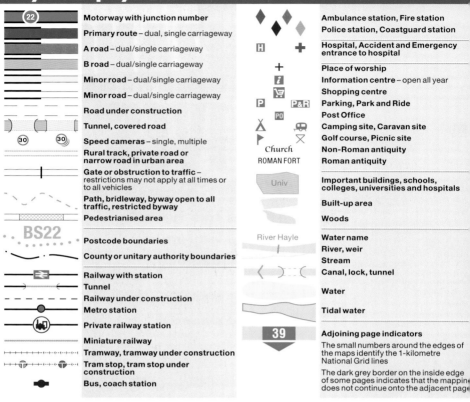

	Motorway with junction number
	Primary route – dual, single carriageway
	A road – dual/single carriageway
	B road – dual/single carriageway
	Minor road – dual/single carriageway
	Minor road – dual/single carriageway
	Road under construction
	Tunnel, covered road
	Speed cameras – single, multiple
	Rural track, private road or narrow road in urban area
	Gate or obstruction to traffic – restrictions may not apply at all times or to all vehicles
	Path, bridleway, byway open to all traffic, restricted byway
	Pedestrianised area
BS22	Postcode boundaries
	County or unitary authority boundaries
	Railway with station
	Tunnel
	Railway under construction
	Metro station
	Private railway station
	Miniature railway
	Tramway, tramway under construction
	Tram stop, tram stop under construction
	Bus, coach station

	Ambulance station, Fire station
	Police station, Coastguard station
H	Hospital, Accident and Emergency entrance to hospital
+	Place of worship
i	Information centre – open all year
	Shopping centre
P P&R	Parking, Park and Ride
PO	Post Office
	Camping site, Caravan site
	Golf course, Picnic site
Church	Non-Roman antiquity
ROMAN FORT	Roman antiquity
Univ	Important buildings, schools, colleges, universities and hospitals
	Built-up area
	Woods
River Hayle	Water name
	River, weir
	Stream
	Canal, lock, tunnel
	Water
	Tidal water
39	Adjoining page indicators

The small numbers around the edges of the maps identify the 1-kilometre National Grid lines

The dark grey border on the inside edge of some pages indicates that the mapping does not continue onto the adjacent page

The map scale on the pages numbered in green is 2¼ inches to 1 mile
2.1 cm to 1 km • 1:28 160

0	½ mile	1 mile
0	500m	1km	1500m	2km

The map scale on the pages numbered in blue is 4½ inches to 1 mile
4.2 cm to 1 km • 1:14 080

0	¼ mile	½ mile
0	250m	500m	750m	1km

Abbreviations

Acad	Academy	Ind Est	Industrial Estate	Meml	Memorial	Ret Pk	Retail Park
Allot Gdns	Allotments	IRB Sta	Inshore Rescue Boat Station	Mon	Monument	Sch	School
Cemy	Cemetery			Mus	Museum	Sh Ctr	Shopping Centre
C Ctr	Civic Centre	Inst	Institute	Obsy	Observatory	TH	Town Hall/House
CH	Club House	Ct	Law Court	Pal	Royal Palace	Trad Est	Trading Estate
Coll	College	L Ctr	Leisure Centre	PH	Public House	Univ	University
Crem	Crematorium	LC	Level Crossing	Recn Gd	Recreation Ground	W Twr	Water Tower
Ent	Enterprise	Liby	Library			Wks	Works
Ex H	Exhibition Hall	Mkt	Market	Resr	Reservoir	YH	Youth Hostel

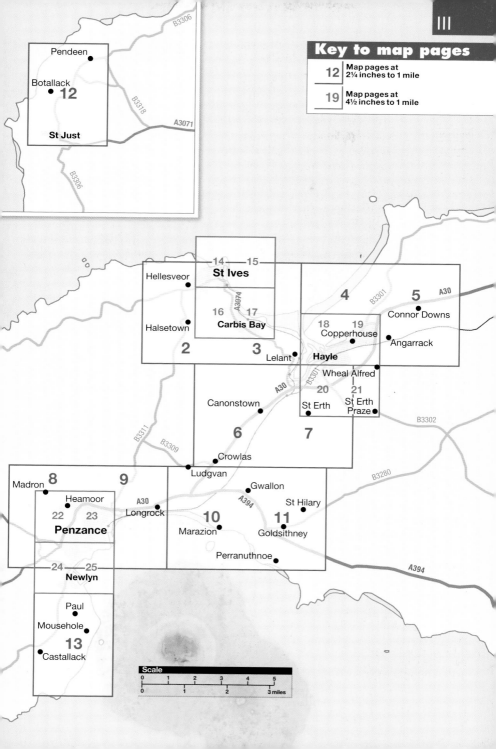

Key to map pages

| 12 | Map pages at 2¼ inches to 1 mile |
| 19 | Map pages at 4½ inches to 1 mile |

B3306

Pendeen
Botallack
12
St Just

B3318

A3071

B3306

Hellesveor

14 — 15
St Ives

A3074

16   17
Halsetown
Carbis Bay

2   **3**
Lelant

4   B3301   **5**   A30

18   19
Copperhouse   Connor Downs

Angarrack

Hayle

Wheal Alfred

20   21
St Erth   St Erth
Praze

B3302

B3301

A30

Canonstown

6   **7**
St Erth

B3311

B3309

Crowlas

Ludgvan

Madron   **8**   **9**

Heamoor

22   23   A30
Longrock
Penzance

24 — 25
Newlyn

Gwallon

A394

St Hilary

10   **11**
Marazion   Goldsithney

Perranuthnoe

A394

B3280

Paul

Mousehole   **13**

Castallack

Scale

0   1   2   3   4   5

0   1   2   3 miles

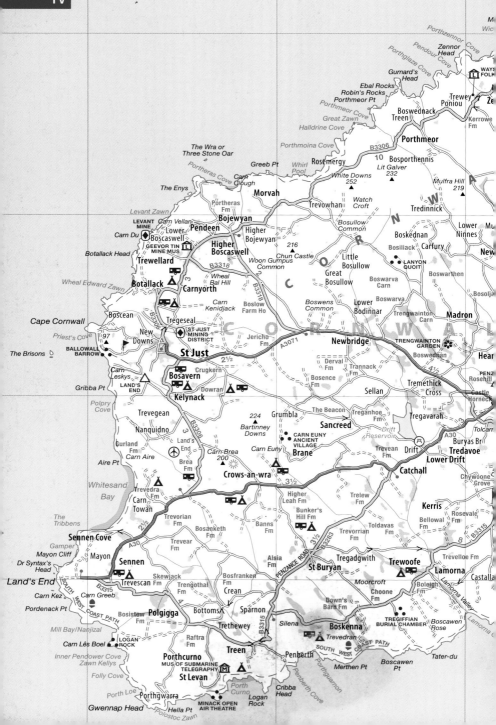

ST IVES BAY

St Ives

ST IVES HEAD or
The Island

Clodgy Pt

Pen Enys Pt

Hor Pt

Peter's Pt

TATE GALLERY

BARBARA HEPWORTH MUS

SOUTH WEST COAST PATH

Trevalgan

Hellesveor

Penbeagle

Ind Est

Porthminster Pt

CARBIS BAY

SOUTH WEST COAST

B3301

A30

Pulsack Manor

Ventonleague

Connor Downs

Angarrack

Rosewall Hill

247

Trendrine Hill

ngleton Downs

Trevessa Fm

The Towans

Phillack

Copperhouse

Gwinear

Higher Bussow Fm

Balnoon

Halsetown

Carbis Bay

Longstone

Lelant

PORT OF HAYLE

Foundry

High Lanes

Hayle

HAYLE PARADISE PARK

Wheal Alfred

Breja

Amalveor

malveor Downs

Trewartha

B3311

Trink Hill 212

ST IVES ROAD

PORT OF LELANT

Trethingey Fm

Tregotha Fm

Amalwhidden Fm

Amalveor

Amalebra

Cripplesease

Trencrom

Lelant Downs

LELANT SALTING

Treva Croft Wood

HAYLE ESTUARY

RSPB

Joppa

St Erth Praze

Calloose

Deveral

Downs

Nancledra

Georgia

Brunnion

Polpeor

130

Ninnes Bridge

TRENCROM HILL

Rose-an-Grouse

Chenhalls

St Erth

4

CALAIS ROAD

B3302

Carzise

Trenowin Downs

Ashtown Fm

Whitecross

Canon's Town

Tregenhorne

Treven

Fraddam

Leedstown

CHYSAUSTER ANCIENT VILLAGE

Castle Gate

Nanceddan

Tregender Manor

Cockwells

3½

Keskeys

TREGONNING & GWINEAR MINING DISTRICT

Townshend

Hellangove Fm

CASTLE ROAD

Trevorrow Fm

Trevessa Fm

Kerthen Wood

Noonvares

Trezelah

Badger's Cross

Treassowe Manor

Vellanoweth

A30

Frythens

Carbows

BOSENCE ROAD

B3280

River Hayle

Tregembo

Godolphin Hill 162

GODOLPHIN HOUSE

Rosemorran Fm

Tolver

Ludgvan

Crowlas

Truthwall

Tregilliowe Fm

Relubbus

Varfell

Trevarthian Fm

5½

Trescowe

gga

Trevarrack

Gulval

2½

A394

Plain-an-Gwarry

St Hilary

Halamanning

Millpool

Boscreege

Balwest

194

Cas Pen

Tres

Longrock

Gwallon

Tregurtha Downs

Goldsithney

Higher Downs

Colenso

Tresowes Green

MARAZION MARSH

RSPB

Perran Downs

B3280

nzance

y Town

Marazion

ST MICHAELS MOUNT

Trenow Cove

Rosudgeon

Kenneggy Downs

Newtown

A394

Germoe

Pengersick

Perranuthnoe

Kenneggy

Maen-du-Point

Trevean Cove

Praa Sands

Rinsey Croft

TRINITY HOUSE NATIONAL LIGHTHOUSE CENTRE

Gwavas Lake

oskilly

Penlee Pt

ousehole

Clement's Isle

n Rock ousehole niard

Stackhouse Cove

Prussia Cove

Cudden Pt

Piskies Cove

Bessy's Cove

Hoe Pt

Praa Sands

Hendra

Rinsey

Rinsey Head

Trewavas Head

RY'S 2:40 (OF SCILLY)

NOV)

MOUNT'S BAY

Scale

0   1   2   3   4km

0   1   2 miles

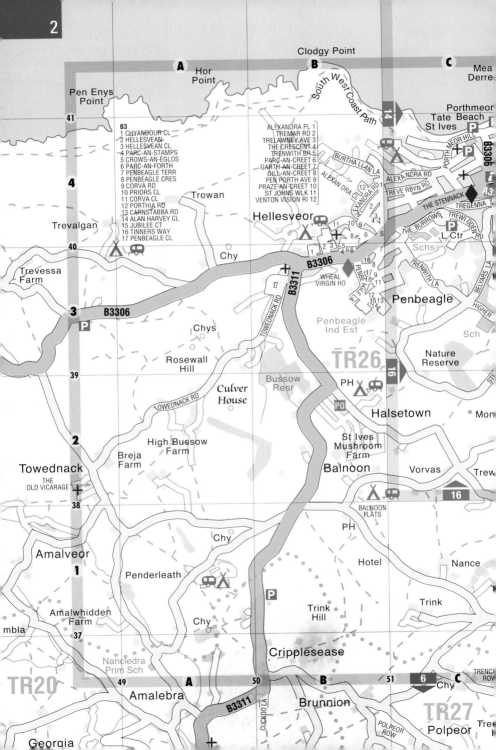

Clodgy Point

A   Hor   B   C   Mea
     Point   Derre

Pen Enys
Point

41

Porthmeor
Tate Beach
St Ives

B3306

B3
1 CHYANDOUR CL
2 HELLESVEAN
3 HELLESVEAN CL
4 PARC-AN-STAMPS
5 CROWS-AN-EGLOS
6 PARC-AN-FORTH
7 PENBEAGLE TERR
8 PENBEAGLE CRES
9 CORVA RD
10 PRIORS CL
11 CORVA CL
12 PORTHIA RD
13 CARNSTABBA RD
14 ALAN HARVEY CL
15 JUBILEE CT
16 TINNERS WAY
17 PENBEAGLE CL

ALEXANDRA PL 1
TREMAR RD 2
TRELAWNEY AVE 3
THE CRESCENT 4
TRENWITH BR 5
PARC-AN-CREET 6
GARTH-AN-CREET 7
GILL-AN-CREET 8
PEN PORTH AVE 9
PRAZE-AN-CREET 10
ST JOHNS WLK 11
VENTON VISION RI 12

Trowan

Trevalgan

40

Hellesveor

Chy

B3306

ALEXANDRA RD
TREVE RBYN RD
THE STENNACK
Tregenna

A3

BURTHA LLAN LA

ALEXAN DRA CL

THE BURROWS
TRENWITH LA
L Ctr
Schs

Trevessa
Farm

B3306

B3311

Wheal
Virgin Ho

PENBEAGLE

Penbeagle

BELYARS LA

HIGHER
Sch

3   B3306

P

Chys

TOWEDNACK RD

Penbeagle
Ind Est

TR26

16

Nature
Reserve

39

Rosewall
Hill

Culver
House

Bussow
Resr

PH

P0

Halsetown   Mon

TOWEDNACK RD

2

Towednack
THE
OLD VICARAGE

38

Breja
Farm

High Bussow
Farm

St Ives
Mushroom
Farm

Balnoon

Vorvas   Trew

16

BALNOON
FLATS

Amalveor

1

Penderleath

Chy

PH

Hotel

Nance

Amalwhidden
Farm

Chy

P

Trink
Hill

Trink

mbla

37

Chy

TR20

49   A   50   B   51   6   Chy   TRENC
ROW

Amalebra

B3311

Brunnion

Polpeor   Tre

Georgia

CUCKOO LA

POLPEOR
ROW

TR27

Polpeor

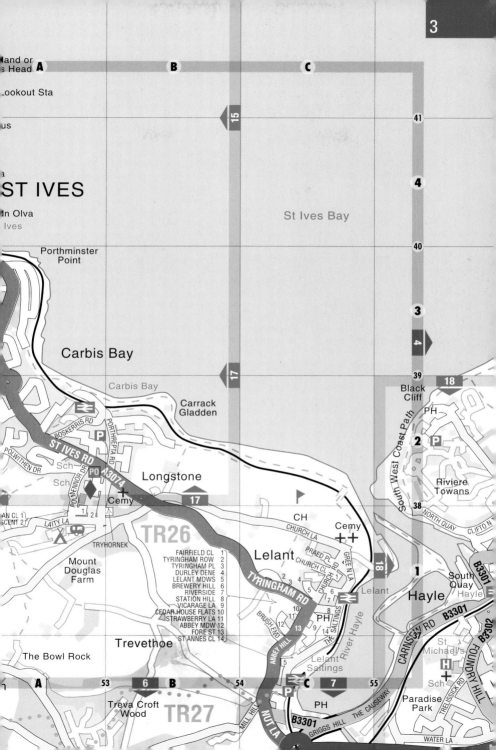

A land or s Head
Lookout Sta
us

ST IVES

n Olva
Ives

St Ives Bay

Porthminster Point

Carbis Bay

Carbis Bay

Carrack Gladden

Black Cliff

PH

South West Coast Path

Riviere Towans

BOSKERRIS RD
ST IVES RD
A3074
POLWITHEN DR
POLMENNOR DR
Sch
PO
Sch
Longstone
Cemy
LAITY LA
TRYHORNEK
AN CL
CENT
Mount Douglas Farm

TR26

NORTH QUAY
CLIFTO

Lelant

CH
CHURCH LA
Cemy
PRAED PL
CHURCH CL
GREEN LA
CHURCH LA

FAIRFIELD CL 1
TYRINGHAM ROW 2
TYRINGHAM PL 3
DURLEY DENE 4
LELANT MDWS 5
BREWERY HILL 6
RIVERSIDE 7
STATION HILL 8
VICARAGE LA 9
CEDAR HOUSE FLATS 10
STRAWBERRY LA 11
ABBEY MDW 12
FORE ST 13
ST ANNES CL 14

TYRINGHAM RD

Lelant

South Quay
Hayle

Hayle

B3301

St Michael's
Sch

FOUNDRY HILL
TRELISSICK RD
B3302

Trevethoe

BRUSH END

ABBEY HILL

River Hayle

THE SALTINGS

PH

Lelant Saltings

CARNSEW RD
B3301

The Bowl Rock

A 53 **6** **B** 54

Treva Croft Wood

TR27

MILL LA
NUT LA

C **7** 55

PH

B3301
GRIGGS HILL
THE CAUSEWAY

Paradise Park

WATER LA

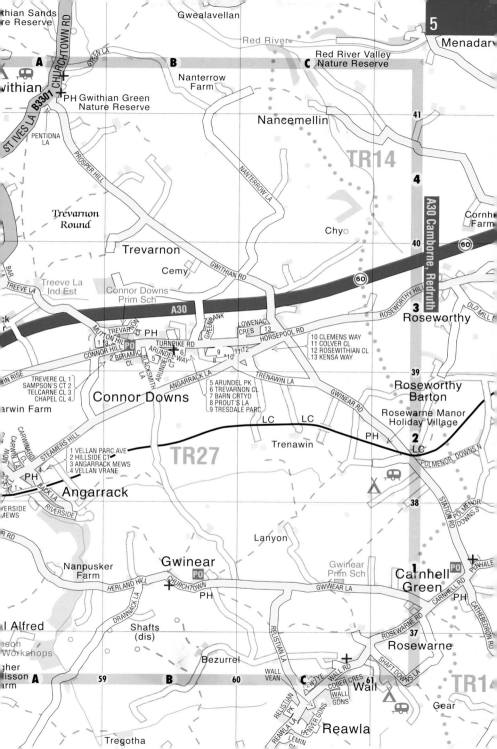

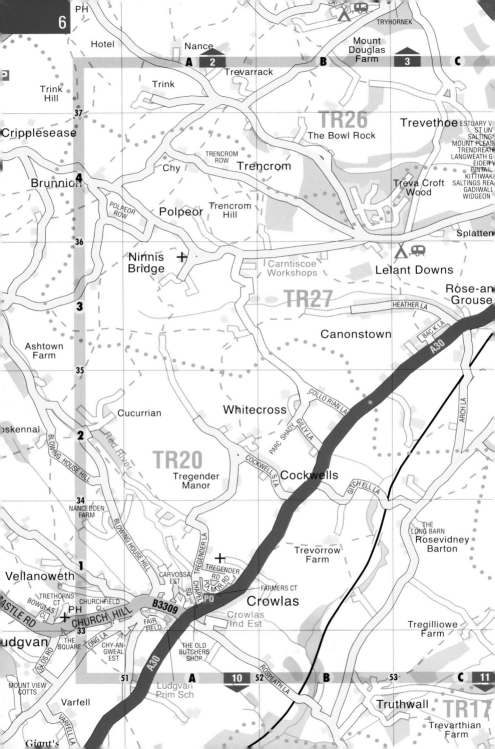

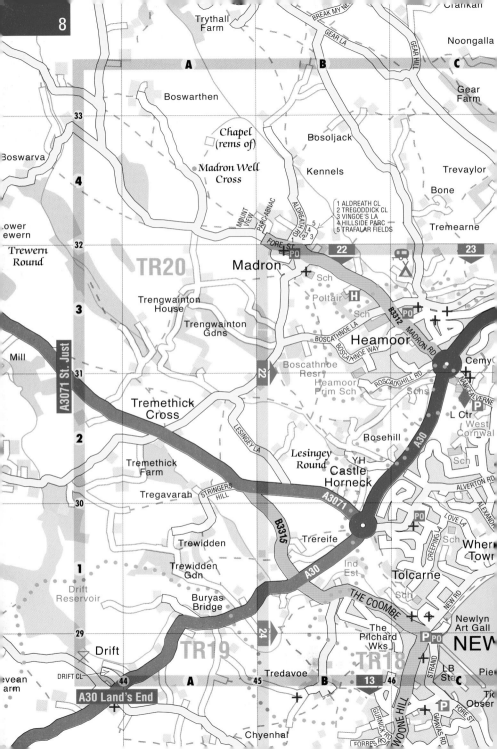

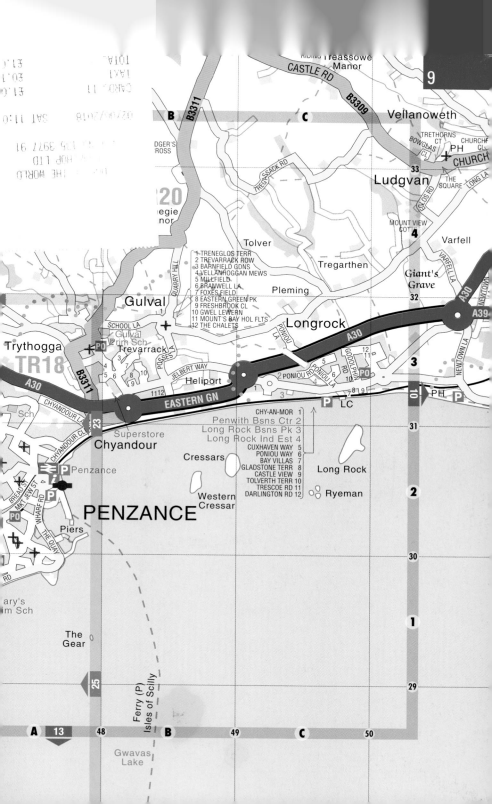

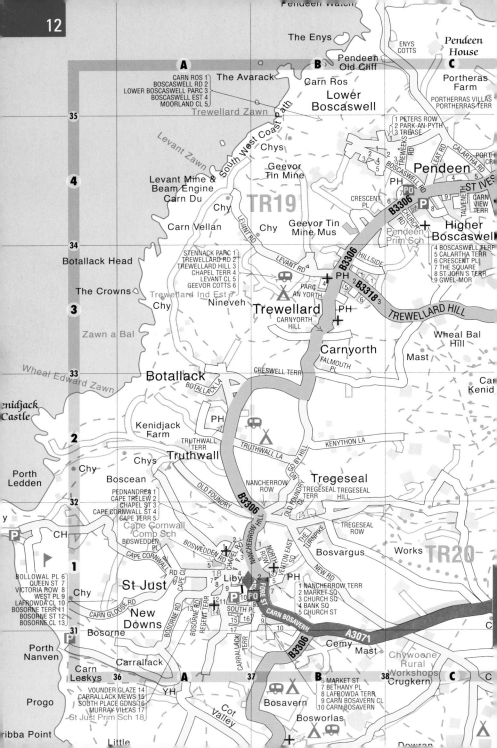

R20
edavoe

NEWLYN
Pier

LB
Sta
STRAND

Tidal
Observatory

25

Gwavas
Lake

P

A **8**

GURNICK RD

CHYWOONE HILL

GWAVAS RD

B

9

C

FORBES

Hotel

24

TR18

TREWARVENETH
FARM COTTS

28

CHYWOONE
GROVE

GWAVAS

Skilly

ROSKILLY
COTTS

1 ST POL DE LEON VIEW
2 TRUNGLE TERR
3 TRUNGLEMOOR COTTS
4 TRUNGLE PARC
5 BOSLANDEW HILL

25

4

Paul

2

Roskilly

CLIFF RD

3

4

Meml

27

Cemy

5

Penlee
Point

QUARRY LA

PH

PARC AN GATE

MOUSEHOLE LA

CLIFF LA

THE PARADE

Sheffield

LONG
ROW

LOWER
SHEFFIELD

Mousehole
Prim Sch

Trevithal

1

2

3

5
6

LOW
LEE RD

P

PH

1 PARADE HILL
2 CARN TODDEN

3

B3315

8
14 9 10
13 11
12
16 15 18
17 19

P

PO

KEIGWEN
PL

Mousehole

St Clements
Isle

Halwyn
Farm

MOUNT
PLEASANT
TERR

LOVE LA

20
21 23 22
24

26

FOUR LANES
END

Raginnis

25 26 27

Merlin Rock

The Mousehole

RAGINNIS HILL

TR19

Point Spaniard

B3
1 LYNWOOD COTTS
2 PREVENNA RD
3 GWELENYS RD
4 PARKRYN RD
5 FOXES LA
6 MARCWHEAL
7 DUMBARTON TERR
8 SOUTHVIEW TERR
9 DUCK ST
10 COMMERCIAL RD
11 QUAY ST
12 NORTH CLIFF
13 FORE ST
14 NORTH ST
15 CHERRY GDN ST
16 VIRGIN PL
17 BROOK ST
18 SOUTH CLIFF
19 GRENFELL ST
20 MILL LA
21 CHAPEL ST
22 THE WHARF
23 PORTLAND PL
24 GURNICK ST
25 RAGINNIS HILL
26 ST CLEMENTS
   TERR
27 SALTPONDS

Castallack

South West Coast Path

2

Penzer Point

25

Kemyel
Crease

1

Slinke Dean

Higher
Kemyel
Farm

Zawn Organ

24

Kemyel Point

morna
Cove

Carn-du

A1
1 AYR CT
2 TREGARTHEN
3 SOUTHFIELDS PL
4 WINDSOR TERR
5 BULLANS TERR
6 TRERICE RD
7 CARNELLS RD
8 NANJIVEY PL
9 NANJIVEY TERR
10 BOSTENNACK PL
11 BOSTENNACK TERR
12 PEARCE'S LA
13 MIDDLE STENNACK COTTS
14 STENNACK GDNS
15 SANDOWS LA
16 ROSEWALL COTTS
17 ROSEWALL TERR
18 FERN GLEN
19 LITTLE-IN-SIGHT

B1
1 ST ANDREW'S ST
2 REDFERN CT
3 STREET-AN-POL
4 TREGENNA PL
5 GABRIEL ST
6 BEDFORD PL
7 WESLEY PL
8 WINDSOR HILL
9 DRILLFIELD LA
10 ALMA TERR
11 TRENWITH TERR
12 NORTH TERR
13 UMFULLA PL
14 TRENWITH PL
15 DOVE ST
16 TREGENNA HILL
17 STREET-AN-GARROW
18 SKIDDEN HILL
19 FERN LEE TERR
20 SEA VIEW TERR
21 ALBERT PL
22 PADNOVER TERR
23 PORTHMINSTER TERR
24 PETES PL
25 CARRACK WIDDEN
26 ALBERT TERR
27 HARLEQUINS
28 ROSEMORRAN
29 TALLAND CT
30 STONES CT

CARTHEW CT 1
CARTHEW TERR 2
AYR TERR 3
WHEEL AYR TERR 4
OCEAN VIEW TERR 5
PARC BEAN TERR 6
BELMONT TERR 7
CHANNEL VIEW 8
VENTNOR TERR 9
BELMONT PL 10
ALEXANDRA ROW 11

1 BEACH CT
2 PORTHGWIDDEN
3 CARNCROWS RD
4 CARNCROWS ST
5 TEETOTAL ST
6 ST EIA ST
7 BACK RD EAST
8 SEA VIEW PL

Clodgy Point

South West Coast Path

Carrick Du

South West Coast Path

Crowner Rocks

Porthmeor Beach

Tate St Ives (Gallery)

Cemy

BEACH RD

WESTWARD RD

ORANGE LA

BACK RD W

BARNOON HILL

Mean Derrens

The Island or St Ives Head

Lookout Sta

Bamalûz Po

QUAY ST

Pier

Smeaton's Pier

Harbour

WHEAL DREAM

ST IVES

BURTHALLAN LA

TR26

BURTHALLAN LA

CARTHEW WAY

CARTHEW CL.

ALEXANDRA RD

PORTHMEOR HILL

AYR LA

Mus

Pier

LB Sta

FORE ST

HIGH ST

B3306

WHARF RD

PENDOLA WLK

Pedn Olva

Pellesveor

ALEXANDRA CL

ALEXANDRA RD

ALEXANDRA TERR

TREVERBYN RD

BULLAN'S LA

BEDFORD RD

CHAPEL ST

Liby

A3074

WARREN

18/19

PO

St Ives

TRELAWNEY AVE

TRELAWNEY RD

TREGWARY RD

RERICE PL

THE STENNACK

PARK AVE

TREGENNA TERR

BISHOP'S RD

TREWIDDEN RD

BELLERS RD

TALLAND RD

ALBANY TERR

THE TERRACE

Edward Hain Com

Porthminster Beach

HIGHER STENNACK

B3306

THE BURROWS

TRENWITH SQ

L Ctr

St Ives Jun & Inf Schs

Bahavella Farm

PEN-AN-GWEL LA

HIGHER TREWIDDEN RD

BAHAVELLA DR

LANSDOWNE

CAMATE

MAS-TA RD

PRIMROSE VALLEY

GWEL-AN-MOR APARTMENTS

DRAYCOTT TERR

B3306

TRENWITH LA

BELYARS LA

PRIMROSE CT

Hotel

CH

HAIN WK

A3074

'HEAL GIN HO

PENBEAGLE LA

PENWITH RD

PORTHIA

HIGHER BU

TRENWITH LA

BELYARS CT

Penbeagle

A B C

42

4

32 (Page 14)
1 ST NICHOLAS CT
2 SAIL LOFT FLATS
3 THE ROPE WLK
4 ISLAND RD
5 PENAMEYNE CT
6 PORTHMEORE RD
7 BACK RD E
8 THE WHARF
9 FISH ST
0 BETHESDA PL
1 VICTORIA RD
2 VICTORIA PL
3 BARNALOFT
4 PIAZZA
5 NORTH PL
6 ST PETERS ST
7 BACK LA
8 CHURCH PL
9 CHY-AN-CHY
0 BAILEYS LA
1 PORTHMEOR SQ
2 BUNKERS HILL
3 ROSE LA
4 LOVE LA
5 THE DIGEY
6 VIRGIN ST
7 MEADOW FLATS
8 GODREVY TERR
9 BARNOON TERR
0 ACADEMY TERR
1 MARKET STRAND
2 LIFEBOAT HILL
3 MARKET SQ
4 BOWLING GN
5 BOWLING GN TERR
6 CARRACK DHU EST
7 CARRACK DHU
8 BELLAIR TERR
9 MOUNT PLEASANT
0 RICHMOND PL
1 TREWYN FLATS
2 BACK ST
3 ATLANTIC TERR
4 CLODGY VIEW
5 WEST PL
6 THE GALLERIES
7 THE MEADOW
8 CRUSOE FLATS
9 DIGEY FLATS
0 PORTHMEOR STUDIOS
1 PORTHMEOR CT
2 MOUNT ZION
3 WILLS LA

3

41

2

1

40

minster

A 53 B C 54

17

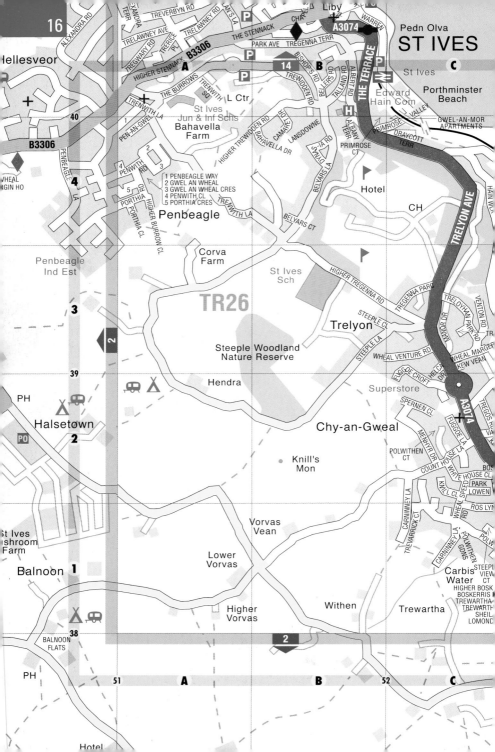

ST IVES

Pedn Olva

Hellesveor

ALEXANDRA RD
TREVERBYN RD
AN'S LA
CHAPEL
Liby
WARREN
A3074

TRELAWNEY AVE
THE STENNACK
TREGENNA TERR
PARK AVE
BISHOP'S RD
14
Pedn Olva

TRELAWNEY RD
TRELAWNEY AVE
TRETICK
HIGHER STENNACK
B3306
A

TREGWARY RD
PL

THE BURROWS
TRENWITH SQ
L Ctr
BELYARS RD
TALLAND RD
THE TERRACE
St Ives

40

B3306

St Ives
Jun & Inf Schs
Bahavella
Farm

HIGHER TREWIDDEN RD
LANSDOWNE
CAMARE
DYNAS
BAHAVELLA DR
HIGHER TREGENNA RD

TREWIDDEN RD
ALBANY TERR
Edward
Hain Com

Porthminster
Beach

GWEL-AN-MOR
APARTMENTS

PENWITH RD
PEN-AN-GWEL
PORTHIA RD
HIGHER BURROW CL
TRENWITH LA

1 PENBEAGLE WAY
2 GWEL AN WHEAL
3 GWEL AN WHEAL CRES
4 PENWITH CL
5 PORTHIA CRES

Hotel

CH

WHEAL
VIRGIN HO

4

PENWITH LA

PENBEAGLE LA

PORTHIA CL

Penbeagle

BELYARS LA
BELYARS CT

PRIMROSE
CT
PRIMROSE
DRAYCOTT
TERR

Corva
Farm

St Ives
Sch

HIGHER TREGENNA RD
TREGENNA PARC
TRELOYHAN PARK RD

TRELYON AVE

Penbeagle
Ind Est

3

TR26

VENTON DR
MANOR DR

2

Trelyon

STEEPLE CL
STEEPLE LA

WHEAL MARGE
KEW VEAN

39

Steeple Woodland
Nature Reserve

WHEAL VENTURE RD

HELCA

Superstore

PH

Hendra

Chy-an-Gweal

SPERNEN CL

FLUGGOE CROFT
MENHYR LA
PREGO

PO

Halsetown

2

Knill's
Mon

POLWITHEN
CT

COUNT HOUSE LA
WHITE HOUSE CL
KNILL CL
PARK
LOWEN
ROS LYN

St Ives
Mushroom
Farm

Vorvas
Vean

CARNINNEY LA
TREWARRICK CT
CARNINNEY LA
WHEAL
POLWITHEN
GDNS
POLWI

Balnoon

1

Lower
Vorvas

Carbis
Water

STEEPL
VIEW
CT
HIGHER BOSK
BOSKERRIS
TREWARTHA
TREWARTHA
SHEIL
LOMOND

38

BALNOON
FLATS

Higher
Vorvas

Withen

Trewartha

2

PH

51

A

B

52

C

Hotel

A   B   15   C

St Ives Bay

minster

40

4

3

3

39

Carbis Bay

Barrepta Cove
or Carbis Bay

1 MOONRAKERS
2 GODREVY CT
3 CARBIS BEACH APARTMENTS
4 RIVIERA APARTMENTS
5 GWELANMOR CL

1 HENDRAS CT
2 HEADLAND CT
3 KARENZA CT
4 TOLPEDN FLATS
5 NAMPARA CL
6 PORDENACK CL

Carrack
Gladden

2

BEACH RD

CARRACK GLADDEN

Carbis
Bay

GWEL MARTEN
FLATS

CORNWALLIS

PENTOWAN CT

BOSKERRIS RD

BOSKERRIS CRES

COMPASS
POINT

LOGANS CT

HEADLAND RD

HEADLAND

SEA
URCHIN

5

3 4

2

GWELANMOR RD

HENDRAS PARC

RICHMOND
WAY

1

PORTHREPTA RD

PARK AN GONWYN

KENIDJACK CL

South West Coast Path

TR26

BARGEPTA
CT

ST ANTA
RD

HENDRA VEAN

Gonwin
Farm

1

ENYS
CL

POLTREEN
CL

POLMEOR
CL

POLMENNOR DR

PO

6

LONGSTONE CL

ROACH'S
CT

Longstone

POLDHU
CL

POLGARTH
CL

TEYLA TOR
RD

m

5 4

TREWARTHA CL

TRENCROM LA

Cemy

Motel

HEATHERBELL
GDNS

Longstone

LONGSTONE HILL

T IVES RD

ITY LA

A   53   B   C   54

A3074

CHURCH LA

38

3

Mount
Douglas

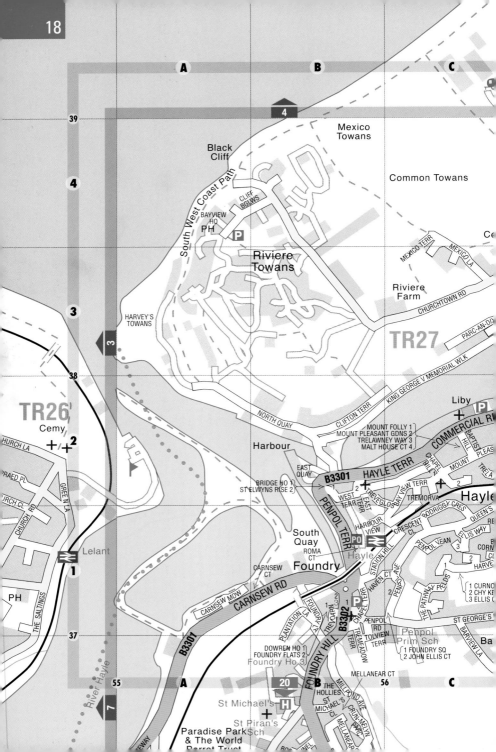

A B C

39

4

Mexico
Towans

Black
Cliff

Common Towans

CLIFF
BGLWS

BAYVIEW
HQ
PH

P

Riviere
Towans

South West Coast Path

MEXICO TERR

MEXICO LA

Ce

3

Riviere
Farm

CHURCHTOWN RD

TR27

PARC-AN-DIX

HARVEY'S
TOWANS

38

KING GEORGE V MEMORIAL WLK

Liby

P

TR26

CLIFTON TERR

COMMERCIAL R

Cemy

2

NORTH QUAY

MOUNT FOLLY 1
MOUNT PLEASANT GDNS 2
TRELAWNEY WAY 3
MALT HOUSE CT 4

BAPTIST

CHAPEL HILL

MOUNT

TRELA

CHURCH LA

Harbour

HILL

PLEAS

HURCH LA

EAST
QUAY

B3301

HAYLE TERR

BAY VIEW TERR

TREMORVA

Hayle

PRAED PL

BRIDGE HO 1
ST ELWYNS RISE 2

WEST
TERR

TREVEGLOS

EAST
TERR

2

BODRIGGY CRES

QUEEN'S

URCH CL

GREEN LA

HARBOUR
VIEW

CRESCENT
CL

PENPOL VEAN

LIS WAY

ST
CORN

URCH RD

South
Quay

PD

Hayle

STATION HILL

3

HARVE

PH

Lelant

ROMA
CT

Foundry

PENPOL TERR

PENPOL AVE

1 CURNO
2 CHY KE
3 ELLIS CT

THE SALTINGS

1

CARNSEW
CT

CARNSEW MDW

CARNSEW RD

CHAPEL TERR

TREVOARTHA

CHAPEL HAVEN

ST GEORGE'S

37

B3301

FOUNDRY HILL

B3302

PENPOL
RD

TOLVIEN
TERR

Penpol
Prim Sch

BARVIEW LA

Ba

PLANTATION LA

FOUNDRY LA

CREMEADOW

1 FOUNDRY SQ
2 JOHN ELLIS CT

55

A

20

H

B

DOWREN HO 1
FOUNDRY FLATS 2
Foundry Ho 3

MELLANEAR CT

56

C

River Hayle

7

St Michael's

THE
HOLLIES

ST
MICHAEL'S
CL

MILLPOND AVE

CRIM KELLY

MELLANEAR

St Piran's

Paradise Park
& The World
Parrot Trust

St Michael's
Sch

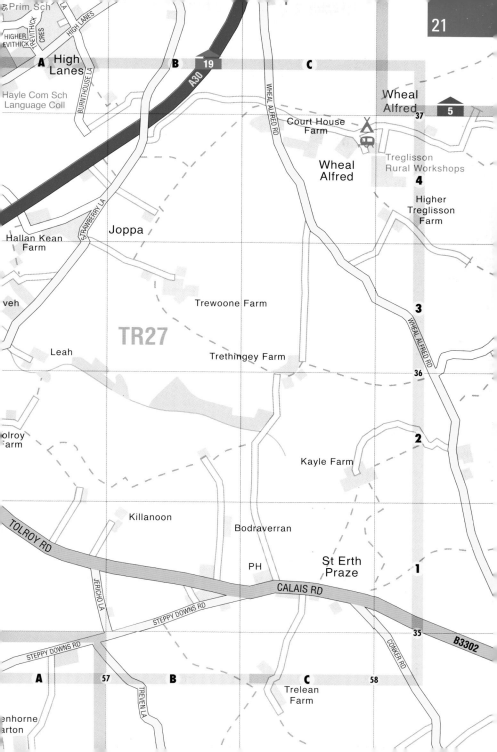

s Prim Sch

HIGHER
REVITHICK

REVITHICK
CRES

High Lanes

A

B

19

C

Hayle Com Sch
Language Coll

A30

Wheal
Alfred

37

5

Court House
Farm

Treglisson
Rural Workshops

Wheal
Alfred

4

WHEAL ALFRED RD

Higher
Treglisson
Farm

STRAWBERRY LA

Joppa

Hallan Kean
Farm

veh

Trewoone Farm

3

WHEAL ALFRED RD

TR27

Leah

Trethingey Farm

36

olroy
arm

2

Kayle Farm

TOLROY RD

Killanoon

Bodraverran

PH

St Erth
Praze

1

JERICHO LA

CALAIS RD

35

B3302

CONNER RD

STEPPY DOWNS RD

STEPPY DOWNS RD

A

57

B

TREVEN LA

C

58

Trelean
Farm

enhorne
arton

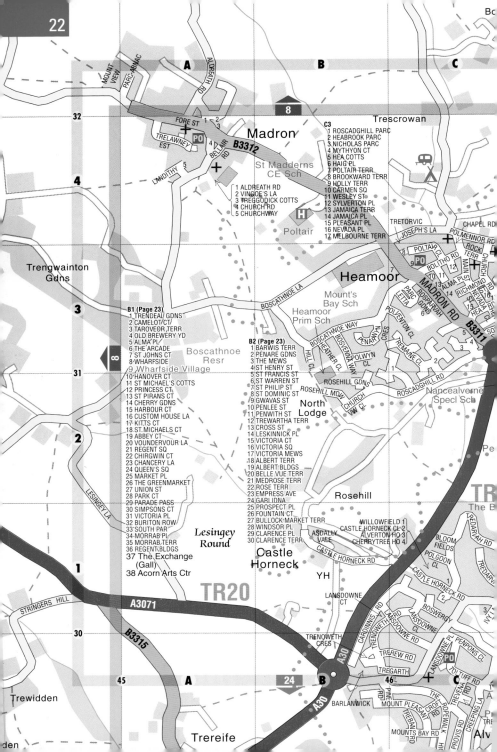

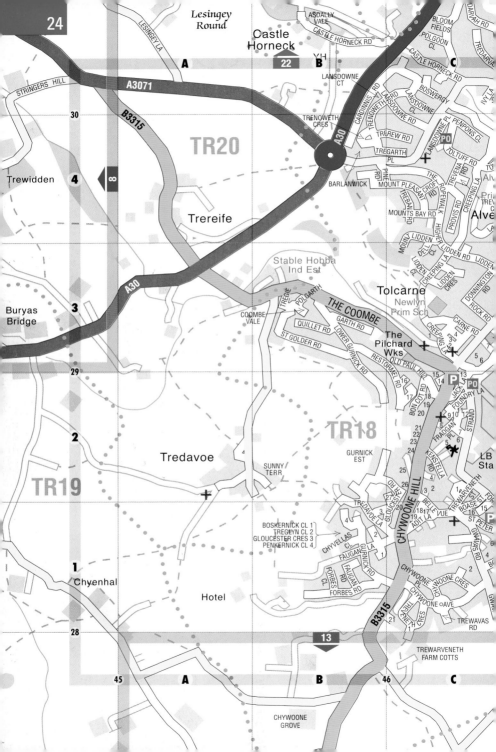

Index

Street names are listed alphabetically and show the locality, the Postcode district, the page number and a reference to the square in which the name falls on the map page

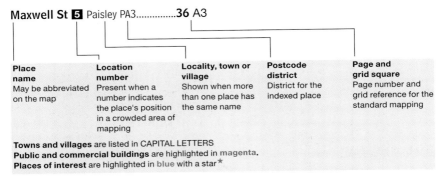

Maxwell St 5 Paisley PA3...............36 A3

Place name	Location number	Locality, town or village	Postcode district	Page and grid square
May be abbreviated on the map	Present when a number indicates the place's position in a crowded area of mapping	Shown when more than one place has the same name	District for the indexed place	Page number and grid reference for the standard mapping

Towns and villages are listed in CAPITAL LETTERS
Public and commercial buildings are highlighted in magenta.
Places of interest are highlighted in blue with a star★

Abbreviations used in the index

Acad	Academy	Ct	Court	Hts	Heights	Pl	Place
App	Approach	Ctr	Centre	Ind	Industrial	Prec	Precinct
Arc	Arcade	Ctry	Country	Inst	Institute	Prom	Promenade
Ave	Avenue	Cty	County	Int	International	Rd	Road
Bglw	Bungalow	Dr	Drive	Intc	Interchange	Recn	Recreation
Bldg	Building	Dro	Drove	Junc	Junction	Ret	Retail
Bsns, Bus	Business	Ed	Education	L	Leisure	Sh	Shopping
Bvd	Boulevard	Emb	Embankment	La	Lane	Sq	Square
Cath	Cathedral	Est	Estate	Liby	Library	St	Street
Cir	Circus	Ex	Exhibition	Mdw	Meadow	Sta	Station
Cl	Close	Gd	Ground	Meml	Memorial	Terr	Terrace
Cnr	Corner	Gdn	Garden	Mkt	Market	TH	Town Hall
Coll	College	Gn	Green	Mus	Museum	Univ	University
Com	Community	Gr	Grove	Orch	Orchard	Wk, Wlk	Walk
Comm	Common	H	Hall	Pal	Palace	Wr	Water
Cott	Cottage	Ho	House	Par	Parade	Yd	Yard
Cres	Crescent	Hospl	Hospital	Pas	Passage		
Cswy	Causeway	HQ	Headquarters	Pk	Park		

Index of towns, villages, streets, hospitals, industrial estates, railway stations, schools, shopping centres, universities and places of interest

Abb–Ang

A

Abbey Ct 19 TR18.....23 B1
Abbey Hill TR26.......7 A4
Abbey Mdw TR26......3 C1
Abbey St TR18 ....23 B1
Academy Terr 30
  TR26 ....14 B2
Acorn Arts Ctr★ 38
  TR18...............23 B1
Adelaide St TR18.....23 B2
Adit La TR18 ....24 C1

Alan Harvey Cl 14
  TR26 ....2 B3
Albany Terr TR26 .....16 B4
Albert Bldgs 19 TR18 .23 B2
Albert Pl 21 TR26.....14 B1
Albert Rd TR26.......14 B1
Albert St TR18 ....23 C2
Albert Terr
  18 Penzance TR18.....23 B2
  26 St Ives TR26......14 B1
Albertus Dr TR27.....20 B3
Albertus Gdns TR27 .20 B3
Albertus Rd TR27.....20 B3
Aldreath Cl TR20 .....8 B4
Aldreath Rd TR20 .....8 B4
Alexandra Cl TR26.....2 B4

Alexandra Gdns
  TR18 ....25 A4
Alexandra Ho TR18...25 A3
Alexandra Pl
  Penzance TR18 ....25 A4
  St Ives TR26 ....2 B4
Alexandra Rd
  Penzance TR18 ....25 A4
  St Ives TR26 ....2 B4
Alexandra Terr
  Penzance TR18 ....25 A3
  St Ives TR26 ....14 A1
Alma Pl
  Heamoor TR18.......22 C3
  5 Penzance TR18.....23 B1

Alma Terr
  Penzance TR18 ....23 B1
  10 St Ives TR26.......14 B1
Alverne Bldgs 7
  TR18 ....23 A1
ALVERTON...........24 C4
Alverton Cty Prim Sch
  TR18 ....24 C4
Alverton Ho TR18 ....22 C1
Alverton Rd TR18.....23 A1
Alverton St TR18 .....23 B1
Alverton Terr 4
  TR18 ....23 A1
Amal An Avon TR27...19 B3
ANGARRACK..........5 A2
Angarrack La TR27 ...5 B2

Angarrack Mews TR27 **5** A2
Antoine Cl **4** TR18 . . . **24** C2
Antoine Terr **23**
  TR18 . . . . **24** C2
Arcade The **6** TR18 . . **23** B1
Arch La TR27. . . . . **6** C2
Art Gallery Terr
  TR18 . . . . **24** C3
Arundel Cl TR27. . . . . . . **5** B3
Arundel Pk TR27 . . . . . . **5** B3
Arundel Way TR27 . . . . . **5** B3
Asdally Vale TR18. . . . . **22** B1
Ash Dr TR27 . . . . **20** B3
Ash Gr TR27 . . . . **20** B3
Atlantic Terr **43** TR26 .**14** B2
Avenue The TR20 . . . . . **11** C3
Ayr Ct **1** TR26 . . . . **14** A1
Ayr La TR26 . . . . **14** B2
Ayr Terr TR26 . . . . **14** A2

B

Back La
  Angarrack TR27. . . . . **5** A2
  Marazion TR17. . . . . **10** B2
  St Erth TR27. . . . . **6** C3
  17 St Ives TR26. . . . . **14** B2
Back Road E **7** TR26 .**14** B2
Back Road W TR26 . .**14** B2
Back St **42** TR26 . . . . . . **14** B2
Bahavella Dr TR26. . . .**16** B4
Baileys La **20** TR26. . . .**14** B2
BALNOON **2** B2
Balnoon Flats TR26. . . . **2** B1
Bambry Cl TR20 . . . . . . **11** B2
Bampflyde Way TR20 .**11** C2
Bank Sq TR19 . . . .**12** B1
Baptist Hill TR27 . . . . .**18** C2
Barbara Hepworth Mus
  & Sculpture Gdn ★
  TR26 . . . .**14** B2
Barbican La TR18 . . . .**25** C4
Bar La TR27. . . . . **5** A3
Barlandhu **17** TR18 . . .**24** C2
Barlanwick TR18 . . . . .**24** B4
Barnaloft **13** TR26 . . . .**14** B2
Barn Courtyard TR27 . . **5** B3
Barnfield Gdns TR18. . . **9** B3
Barnoon Hill TR26. . . .**14** B2
Barnoon Terr **29**
  TR26 . . . .**14** B2
Barrepta Cl TR26 . . . . .**17** A1
Barton Cl TR18. . . . . . .**23** A3
Barview La TR27 . . . . . .**20** C4
Barwis Hill TR18 . . . . .**23** B2
Barwis Terr **1** TR18 . .**23** B2
Battery Mill La TR27. . . . **7** A2
Battery Rd TR18. . . . . .**25** C4
Bayview Ho TR27. . . . .**18** A4
Bay View Terr
  Hayle TR27. . . . .**18** C2
  26 Newlyn TR18 . . . . . .**24** C2
  Penzance TR18 . . . .**25** A4
Bay Villas TR20 . . . . **9** C3

Beach Ct TR26 . . . .**14** C2
Beachfield Ct TR18. . .**25** A4
Beach Rd
  Carbis Bay TR26 . . . . . .**17** A2
  St Ives TR26 . . . .**14** A2
Beacon Rd TR17. . . . . .**10** B2
Beatrice Terr TR27. . . .**19** A3
Bedford Pl **6** TR26 . .**14** B1
Bedford Rd TR26 . . . . .**14** B1
Belgravia St TR18 . . . .**23** B1
Bellair Rd TR20 . . . . . .**22** A4
Bellair Terr **38** TR26. . .**14** B2
Belle Vue TR18 . . . .**24** C1
Belle Vue Terr **20**
  TR18 . . . .**23** B2
Belliers La TR26. . . . . .**14** B1
Belmont Pl TR26 . . . . .**14** A2
Belmont Terr TR26 . . .**14** A2
Belvedere La TR20 . . .**11** C2
Belyars Ct TR26 . . . . . .**16** B4
Belyars La TR26 . . . . . .**16** B4
Beramic Cl TR27 . . . . . . **5** B3
Bethany Pl TR19. . . . . .**12** B1
Bethesda Pl **10** TR26 . .**14** B2
Beverley Cres TR27. . .**19** B3
Birch Gr TR27. . . . .**20** B3
Bishop's Rd TR26. . . . .**14** B1
Black Rd TR27 . . . .**19** A3
Blacksmith La TR27 . . . **5** B3
Bloom Fields TR18 . . .**22** C1
Blowing House Hill
  TR20 . . . . **6** A1
Boase St TR18 . . . .**24** C1
Bodriggy Cres TR27 . .**18** C1
Bodriggy Ct TR27 . . . .**19** A2
Bodriggy Prim Sch
  TR27 . . . .**19** A1
Bodriggy St TR27. . . . .**19** A2
Bodriggy Villas TR27 . .**19** A2
Bolitho Rd TR18. . . . . .**22** C3
Bolitho Sch The
  TR18 . . . .**22** C1
Bollowal Pl TR19 . . . . .**12** A1
Boltern Rd TR17. . . . . .**10** C2
Bon Cot Rd TR18 . . . . .**24** C2
Bon Villas **18** TR18 . . . .**24** C2
Boscarnek TR27. . . . . .**20** A1
Boscaswell Downs
  TR19 . . . .**12** C4
Boscaswell Est TR19. .**12** B4
Boscaswell Rd TR19 . .**12** C4
Boscaswell Terr
  TR19 . . . .**12** C4
Boscathnoe La TR18. .**22** B3
Boscathnoe Way
  TR18 . . . .**22** B3
Boskennel Dr TR27 . . .**20** B4
Boskenza Ct TR26 . . . .**16** C2
Boskernick Cl TR18. . .**24** B1
Boskerris Cres TR26 . .**17** A2
Boskerris Mews
  TR26 . . . .**17** A1
Boskerris Rd TR26. . . .**17** A2
Boslandew Hill TR19 .**13** B4

Bosorne Cl TR19 . . . . .**12** A1
Bosorne Rd TR19. . . . .**12** A1
Bosorne St TR19 . . . . .**12** A1
Bosorne Terr TR19. . . .**12** A1
Bostennack Pl **10**
  TR26 . . . .**14** A1
Bostennack Terr **11**
  TR26 . . . .**14** A1
Bosvenna Way TR18 . .**22** B3
Boswedden Pl TR19 . .**12** A1
Boswedden Rd TR19. .**12** A1
Boswergy TR18 . . . . . .**22** C1
BOTALLACK **12** A2
Botallack La TR19 . . . .**12** A2
Boundary Cl **21** TR18 .**24** C1
Bowjey Ct **9** TR18. . . .**24** C1
Bowjey Hill TR18 . . . . .**24** C1
Bowjey Terr **5** TR18 . .**24** C1
Bowling Gn **34** TR26 . .**14** B2
Bowling Green Ct
  TR27 . . . .**19** A1
Bowling Green Terr **35**
  TR26 . . . .**14** B2
Bownder Dowr TR27. .**20** B3
Brandy La TR20 . . . . . .**11** C1
Branwell La TR18 . . . . . **9** B3
Bread St TR18. . . . .**23** B1
Brewery Hill TR26 . . . . . **3** C1
Bridge Ho TR27 . . . . . .**18** B2
Bridge Ho The **13**
  TR18 . . . .**24** C2
Briton's Hill TR18 . . . .**23** C2
Brook St **17** TR19. . . . .**13** B3
Brookward Terr **8**
  TR18 . . . .**22** C3
Brookway TR27 . . . . . .**19** B3
Brush End TR26 . . . . **3** C1
Buildings The TR20. . .**10** A3
Bullan's La TR26 . . . . .**14** A1
Bullans Terr **5** TR26. .**14** A1
Bullock Market Terr **27**
  TR18 . . . .**23** B2
Bunkers Hill **22** TR26 .**14** B2
Buriton Row **32** TR18 .**23** B1
Burnthouse La TR27. .**19** A1
Burrows The TR26 . . . .**14** A1
Burthallan La TR26. . . . **2** B4

C

Calartha Rd TR19. . . . .**12** C4
Calartha Terr TR19 . . .**12** C4
Caldwells Rd TR18 . . .**23** B2
Camaret Dr TR26 . . . . .**16** B4
Camelot Ct **2** TR18 . .**23** B1
CANONSTOWN **6** B3
Cape Cl TR19 . . . .**12** A1
Cape Cornwall Comp
  Sch TR19 . . . .**12** A1
Cape Cornwall Rd
  TR19 . . . .**12** A1
Cape Cornwall St
  TR19 . . . .**12** A1
Cape Terr TR19. . . . . . .**12** A1

Cape Trelew TR19 . . . .**12** A1
CARBIS BAY **17** A3
Carbis Bay Sta TR26 . .**17** A2
Cardinnis Rd TR18. . . .**22** B1
Carmen Sq **10** TR18. . .**22** C3
Carminowe Cres **8**
  TR18 . . . .**23** A1
Carn Bosavern TR19. .**12** B1
Carn Bosavern Cl
  TR19 . . . .**12** B1
Carncrows Rd TR26 . .**14** C2
Carncrows St TR26 . . .**14** C2
Carnellis Rd **7** TR26 .**14** A1
Carne Rd TR18 . . . .**24** C3
Carne's Bldgs **11**
  TR18 . . . .**25** B4
Carn Gwavas Terr
  TR18 . . . .**25** A1
Carninney La TR26 . . .**16** C1
Carn Ros TR19 . . . .**12** B4
Carnsew Ct TR27 . . . . .**18** B1
Carnsew Mdw TR27 . .**18** A1
Carnsew Rd TR27 . . . .**18** A1
Carnstabba Rd **13**
  TR26 . . . . **2** B3
Carntiscoe Workshops
  TR27 . . . . **6** B3
Carn Todden TR19 . . . .**13** C3
Carn View Terr TR19 . .**12** C4
CARNYORTH **12** B3
Carnyorth Hill TR19 . .**12** B3
Carnyorth Terr TR19 . .**12** B3
Caroline Cl TR27 . . . . .**19** B3
Caroline Row TR27 . . .**19** B3
Carrack Dhu **37** TR26 .**14** B2
Carrack Dhu Est **36**
  TR26 . . . .**14** B2
Carrack Gladden
  TR26 . . . .**17** A2
Carrack Widden **25**
  TR26 . . . .**14** B1
Carrallack Mews
  TR19 . . . .**12** A1
Carthew Cl TR26 . . . . .**14** A2
Carthew Ct TR26 . . . . .**14** A2
Carthew Terr TR26. . . .**14** A2
Carthew Way TR26 . . .**14** A2
Carvossa Est TR20. . . . . **6** A1
Carwinard Cl TR27 . . . . **5** A2
Carwin La TR27 . . . . **5** A2
Carwin Rise
  Angarrack TR27. . . . . **5** A2
  Hayle TR27. . . . .**19** B3
CASTLE HORNECK . .**22** B1
Castle Horneck Cl
  TR18 . . . .**22** C1
Castle Horneck Rd
  TR18 . . . .**22** C1
Castle Rd TR18. . . . . . .**23** B3
Castle View TR20 . . . . . **9** C3
Causewayhead TR18 .**23** B1
Causeway The TR27 . .**20** A4

Cedar House Flats
TR26 . . . . 3 C1
Chalets The TR18 . . . . . . 9 B3
Chancery La 28 TR18 . .23 B1
Channel View TR26 . . .14 A2
Chapel Cl TR27 . . . . 5 B3
Chapel Hill
Hayle TR27 . . . . .18 C2
St Erth TR27 . . . . .20 A1
Chapel La
Goldsithney TR20 . . . . . . .11 C2
Hayle TR27 . . . . .19 A2
Chapel Rd
Heamoor TR18 . . . . . . .22 C4
St Just TR19 . . . . .12 A1
Chapel Sq TR20 . . . . . . 6 A1
Chapel St
Marazion TR17 . . . . . . .10 B2
21 Mousehole TR19 . . . .13 B3
9 Newlyn TR18 . . . . . .24 C2
Penzance TR18 . . . . . . .23 B1
St Ives TR26 . . . . .14 B1
St Just TR19 . . . . .12 A1
Chapel Terr
Hayle TR27 . . . . .18 B1
Trewellard TR19 . . . . . .12 B3
Charles St TR18 . . . . . .24 C3
CHENHALLS 20 A2
Chenhalls Cl TR27 . . . . .7 A3
Chenhalls Rd TR27 . . .20 A2
Cherry Gdns 14 TR18 .23 B1
Cherry Gdn St 15
TR19 . . . . .13 B3
Cherrytree Ho TR18 . .22 C1
Chirgwin Ct 22 TR18 . .23 B1
Chiverton Cl TR20 . . . .11 C1
Chiverton Cross
TR20 . . . . .11 C1
Chiverton Way TR20 . .11 C1
Church Cl TR26 . . . . . . .3 C1
Church La TR26 . . . . . . .3 C1
Church Pl 18 TR26 . . . .14 B2
Church Rd
Heamoor TR18 . . . . . . .22 C3
Lelant TR26 . . . . .3 C1
Madron TR20 . . . . .22 A4
Pendeen TR19 . . . . .12 C4
Church Sq TR19 . . . . . .12 B1
Church St
15 Newlyn TR18 . . . . . .24 C1
St Erth TR27 . . . . .20 A1
St Just TR19 . . . . .12 B1
Churchtown TR27 . . . . . 5 B1
Churchtown Rd TR27 .18 C3
Church View Cl TR18 . .22 B2
Churchway
Madron TR20 . . . . .22 A4
11 Marazion TR17 . . . . .10 C2
Chy-an-Chy 19 TR26 .14 B2
Chyanclare TR18 . . . . .23 A2
Chyandaunce Cl
TR18 . . . . .23 C4

Chyandaunce Terr
TR18 . . . . .23 C4
CHYANDOUR 23 C3
Chyandour Cl 1 TR26 . 2 B3
Chyandour Cliff
TR18 . . . . .23 C2
Chyandour La TR18 . . .23 C3
Chyandour Sq TR18 . .23 C3
Chyandour Terr
TR18 . . . . .23 C3
Chy an Dowr TR27 . . .19 B3
CHY-AN-GWEAL 16 B2
Chy-an-Gweal Est
TR20 . . . . .10 A4
Chy-an-Hall TR18 . . . .23 C4
Chy-an-Mor TR20 . . . . .9 C3
Chy Cober TR27 . . . . .19 B3
Chycornick Terr
TR18 . . . . .23 C4
Chy Kensa Cl TR27 . . .18 C1
Chynance TR18 . . . . . .25 A4
Chynoweth Gdns
TR18 . . . . .23 C4
Chynoweth La TR20 . . .11 C3
Chyvellas Cl TR18 . . . .24 B1
Chywoone Ave TR18 . .24 C1
Chywoone Cres TR18 24 C1
Chywoone Hill TR18 . .24 C1
Chywoone Pl TR18 . . . .24 C1
Clarence Pl 29 TR18 . .23 B2
Clarence St TR18 . . . . .23 B1
Clarence Terr 30
TR18 . . . . .23 B2
Cledma Bank TR27 . . .20 A2
Clemens Way TR27 . . . 5 B3
Clements Rd TR18 . . . .23 A1
Cliff Bglws TR27 . . . . .18 A4
Cliff La TR19 . . . . .13 C3
Cliff Rd
Mousehole TR19 . . . . .13 C4
Newlyn TR18 . . . . .25 A1
Clifton Hill 14 TR18 . .24 C2
Clifton Terr
Hayle TR27 . . . . .18 B2
15 Newlyn TR18 . . . . . .24 C2
Clodgy View 44 TR26 .14 B2
Close The TR18 . . . . . .23 A3
Coach Ho The TR18 . . .23 C3
Coastguard Cres
TR18 . . . . .23 C2
COCKWELLS 6 B2
Cockwells La TR26 . . . . 6 B2
Coinagehall Pl TR18 . .25 C4
Coinagehall St TR18 . .25 C4
Colenso Cross TR20 . .11 C2
Colinsey Pl TR18 . . . . .23 A3
Colinsey Rd TR18 . . . . .23 A3
Collorian La TR26 . . . . . 6 B2
Collygree Parc TR20 . .11 B2
Col-Moor Cl TR27 . . . .19 B3
Colver Cl TR27 . . . . 5 B3
Commercial Rd
Hayle TR27 . . . . .18 C2
10 Mousehole TR19 . . . .13 B3

Compass Point TR26 .17 A2
CONNOR DOWNS 5 B2
Connor Downs Prim Sch
TR27 . . . . 5 B3
Connor Hill TR27 . . . . . . 5 B3
Coombe La TR18 . . . . .23 A3
Coombe Pk TR18 . . . . .23 B2
Coombe Rd TR18 . . . . .23 B3
Coombe The TR18 . . . .24 B3
Coombe Vale TR18 . . .24 B3
Copper Hill TR27 . . . . .19 A2
COPPERHOUSE 19 A2
Copper Terr TR27 . . . . .19 A3
Cormoran Ct TR17 . . . .10 C2
Cornubia Cl TR27 . . . . .18 C1
Cornwallis TR26 . . . . . .17 B2
Cornwall Terr TR18 . . .25 B4
Coronation Rd TR27 . .19 A1
Corva Cl 11 TR26 . . . . . 2 B3
Corva Rd 9 TR26 . . . . . 2 B3
Coulson's Bldgs 10
TR18 . . . . .25 B4
Coulson's Pl 9 TR18 . .25 B4
Coulson's Terr 8
TR18 . . . . .25 B4
Countess Bridge La
TR27 . . . . 7 C1
Count House La
TR26 . . . . .16 C2
Creeping La
Newlyn TR18 . . . . .24 C3
Penzance TR18 . . . . . . .24 C4
Crescent Cl TR27 . . . . .18 C1
Crescent Pl TR19 . . . . .12 B4
Crescent The
Carbis Bay TR26 . . . . . . .3 A1
St Ives TR26 . . . . .2 B4
Creswell Terr TR19 . . .12 B2
Croft Rd TR18 . . . . .24 C4
Cross St
Hayle TR27 . . . . .19 A2
13 Penzance TR18 . . . . .23 B2
CROWLAS 6 B1
Crowlas Ind Est TR20 . .6 A1
Crows-an-Eglos 5
TR26 . . . . 2 B3
Crun-Melyn Parc
TR27 . . . . .20 B4
Crusoe Flats 48 TR26 .14 B2
Curnows Rd TR27 . . . .18 C1
Custom House Ct
TR18 . . . . .23 C1
Custom House La 16
TR18 . . . . .23 B1
Cuxhaven Way TR20 . . .9 C3

Daniel Pl TR18 . . . . . . .25 B4
Darlington Rd TR20 . . .9 C3
Dell Cl TR18 . . . . .24 C3
Derowen Dr TR27 . . . .20 B3
Digey Flats 49 TR26 . .14 B2
Digey The 25 TR26 . . .14 B2

Dock La TR18 . . . . .23 C1
Dola La TR20 . . . . .11 B2
Donnington Rd TR18 . .24 C3
Dove St 16 TR26 . . . . . .14 B1
Dowren Ho TR27 . . . . .18 B1
Dracaena Ave TR27 . . .19 B2
Dracaena Cres TR27 . .19 B2
Drannack La TR27 . . . . . 5 B1
Draycott Terr TR26 . . .16 C4
Drillfield La 9 TR26 . .14 B1
Duck St 9 TR19 . . . . . .13 B3
Dumbarton Terr 7
TR19 . . . . .13 B3
Durley Dene TR26 . . . . .3 C1
Dynas-Ia Rd TR26 . . . .16 B4

E

East Cliff La TR17 . . . .10 C2
Eastern Gn
Gulval TR18 . . . . .9 B3
Penzance TR18 . . . . . . .23 C3
Eastern Green Pk
TR18 . . . . 9 B3
East Quay TR27 . . . . . .18 B2
East Terr TR27 . . . . .18 B2
Ebenezer Pl 12 TR18 . .24 C1
Eden Gdns 14 TR18 . . .24 C1
Eden Terr 13 TR18 . . . .24 C1
Ednovean La TR20 . . . .11 B1
Edward Hain Com Hospl
TR26 . . . . .14 B1
Egloshayle Rd TR27 . .19 B2
Eglos Rd TR20 . . . . . . .10 A4
Eider Wlk TR27 . . . . 7 A4
Elizabeth Terr TR17 . . .10 B2
Ellis Cl TR27 . . . . .18 C1
Ellis Way TR27 . . . . . . .18 C1
Elms Close Terr 25
TR18 . . . . .24 C2
Elms The TR20 . . . . . . .11 A1
Empress Ave 23
TR18 . . . . .23 B2
Enys Cl TR26 . . . . .17 A1
Estuary View TR26 . . . . 7 A4
Exchange (Gall) The*
37 TR18 . . . . .23 B1

F

Fair Field TR20 . . . . . . .6 A1
Fairfield Cl TR26 . . . . . . 3 C1
Falmouth Pl TR19 . . . .12 B3
Farmers Ct TR20 . . . . . .6 A1
Farmers Mdw 8
TR18 . . . . .24 C2
Farrar Cl TR27 . . . . . . .19 B4
Faugan La TR18 . . . . . .24 B1
Faugan Rd TR18 . . . . . .24 B1
Feliskirk La TR17 . . . . .10 B3
Fern Glen 18 TR26 . . .14 A1
Fern Lee Terr 19
TR26 . . . . .14 B1
Fish St 9 TR26 . . . . . . .14 B2

Florence Pl TR18 . . . . . 24 C3
Forbes Cl TR18 . . . . 24 B1
Forbes Rd TR18 . . . . . . 24 B1
Fore St
 Goldsithney TR20 . . . . . 11 B2
 Hayle TR27 . . . . 19 A2
 Lelant TR26 . . . . 3 C1
 Madron TR20 . . . . 8 B4
 Marazion TR17 . . . . 10 C2
 13 Mousehole TR19 . . . 13 B3
 Newlyn TR18 . . . . 24 C1
 St Erth TR27 . . . . 20 A1
 St Ives TR26 . . . . 14 B2
 St Just TR19 . . . . 12 B1
Forreglos Dr **10**
 TR17 . . . . 10 C2
Forth an Streth TR27 . 19 B3
Forth an Tewennow
 TR27 . . . . 19 A3
Forth-an-Tre TR27 . . . 19 A3
Forth an Ula TR27 . . . 19 B3
FOUNDRY 18 B1
Foundry Flats TR27 . . 18 B1
Foundry Hill TR27 . . . 20 B4
Foundry Ho TR27 . . . . 18 B1
Foundry La
 Hayle TR27 . . . . 18 B1
 Newlyn TR18 . . . . 24 C2
Foundry Sq TR27 . . . . 18 B1
Fountain Ct **26** TR18 . 23 B2
Foxes Field TR18 . . . . . 9 B3
Foxes La **5** TR18 . . . . 13 B3
Fradgan Pl TR18 . . . . 24 C2
Fradgan The **12** TR18 . 24 C2
Franwill Terr **16**
 TR18 . . . . 24 C1
Freshbrook Cl TR18 . . 9 B3
Fuggoe Croft TR26 . . . 16 C3
Fuggoe La TR26 . . . . . 16 C2

G

Gabriel St **5** TR26 . . . . 14 B1
Gadiwall Rise TR27 . . . 7 A4
Galleries The **46**
 TR26 . . . . 14 B2
Garlidna TR18 . . . . 23 B2
Garth-an-Creet TR26 . . 2 B4
Garth Rd TR18 . . . . . . 24 B3
Gateway Ct TR27 . . . . . 7 A3
Gears La TR17, TR20 . . 11 A4
Geevor Cotts TR19 . . . 12 B3
Geevor Tin Mine Mus★
 TR19 . . . . 12 B4
Gill-an-Creet TR26 . . . 2 B4
Gilly La TR26 . . . . 6 B2
Gitchell La
 Crowlas TR20 . . . . 6 B1
 St Erth TR26 . . . . 6 B2
Gladstone Terr TR20 . . 9 C3
Glebe Row TR27 . . . . . 19 A3
Gloucester Cres
 TR18 . . . . 24 B1

Gloucester Pl **27**
 TR18 . . . . 24 C2
Gloucester Rd TR18 . . 24 C2
Godolphin Ave TR17 . . 10 B2
Godolphin Cl TR17 . . 10 B3
Godolphin Dr TR17 . . 10 B2
Godolphin Pl TR17 . . 10 B2
Godolphin Rd TR20 . . . 9 C3
Godolphin Terr TR17 . . 10 B2
Godrevy Ct TR26 . . . . . 17 A2
Godrevy Terr **28**
 TR26 . . . . 14 B2
GOLDSITHNEY 11 A2
Greeb Way TR20 . . . . . 11 A1
Greenbank
 Connor Downs TR27 . . . . 5 B3
 1 Penzance TR18 . . . . . 23 A1
Green La
 Lelant TR26 . . . . 3 C1
 Marazion TR17 . . . . 10 B3
Green Lane Hill TR18 . 23 C4
Green Lane W TR17 . . 10 B3
Green La The TR27 . . . . 7 B2
Greenmarket The **26**
 TR18 . . . . 23 B1
Green Parc Rd TR27 . . 19 A1
Green St TR18 . . . . 25 C4
Grenfell St **16** TR19 . . 13 B3
Griggs Hill TR27 . . . . . . 7 A4
Grist La TR27 . . . . 5 A2
Grove La TR20 . . . . . . 11 C2
GUILDFORD 19 B2
Guildford Rd TR27 . . . 19 B3
Guildford Road Ind Est
 TR27 . . . . 19 B2
GULVAL 9 B3
Gulval Almshouses
 TR18 . . . . 23 C4
Gulval Cross TR18 . . . 23 C4
Gulval Prim Sch TR18 . . 9 B3
Gurnick Est TR18 . . . . 24 B2
Gurnick Rd TR18 . . . . 24 B1
Gurnick St **24** TR19 . . 13 B3
GWALLON 10 C3
Gwallon La TR17 . . . . 10 C3
Gwarth an Dre TR27 . . 19 B4
Gwavas Bglws **4**
 TR18 . . . . 24 C1
Gwavas La TR18 . . . . . 13 B4
Gwavas Quay **7**
 TR18 . . . . 24 C2
Gwavas Rd TR18 . . . . 24 C1
Gwavas St **9** TR18 . . 23 B2
Gweal Gollas TR27 . . . 19 B4
Gwedhennek TR18 . . . 23 C3
Gwel-an-mor **1**
 TR17 . . . . 10 C2
Gwel-an-mor
 Apartments TR26 . . . 16 C4
Gwelanmor Cl TR26 . . 17 A2
Gwelanmor Dr TR26 . . 17 A2
Gwel an Wheal TR26 . 16 A4
Gwel an Wheal Cres
 TR26 . . . . 16 A4

Gwelenys Rd **3** TR19 . 13 B3
Gwel Lewern TR18 . . . . 9 B3
Gwel Marten Flats
 TR26 . . . . 17 B2
Gwel-Mor TR19 . . . . . 12 C4
Gwel-Tek TR27 . . . . . . 19 A4
Gwel Trencrom TR27 . 20 B3
GWINEAR 5 B1
Gwinear La TR27 . . . . . 5 C1
Gwinear Prim Sch
 TR27 . . . . 5 C1
Gwinear Rd TR27 . . . . . 5 C2
Gwithian Rd TR27 . . . . 5 B3

H

Haig Pl **6** TR18 . . . . . 22 C3
Hain Wlk TR26 . . . . . . 16 C4
HALSETOWN 2 B2
Hamilton Cl TR27 . . . . 20 B4
Hanover Ct TR18 . . . . 23 B1
Harbour Ct **15** TR18 . . 23 B1
Harbour Lights **11**
 TR18 . . . . 24 C1
Harbour View
 Hayle TR27 . . . . 18 B1
 Marazion TR17 . . . . 10 B2
Harbour View Cres
 TR18 . . . . 23 B2
Harlequins **27** TR26 . . 14 B1
Harvey's Towans
 TR27 . . . . 18 A3
Harvey's Way TR27 . . 18 C1
Hatch's Hill TR27 . . . . 5 A2
Haven Ct TR27 . . . . . . 18 C1
Hawkins Ct **2** TR18 . . 23 A1
Hawkins Rd TR18 . . . . 23 A1
HAYLE 18 C2
Hayle Com Sch Lang
 Coll TR27 . . . . 19 A1
Hayle Ind Pk TR27 . . . 19 C3
Hayle Sta TR27 . . . . . . 18 B1
Hayle Terr TR27 . . . . . 18 C2
Heabrook Parc **2**
 TR18 . . . . 22 C3
Hea Cl TR18 . . . . 22 C3
Hea Cotts **5** TR18 . . . 22 C3
Headland Cl TR26 . . . 17 B2
Headland Ct TR26 . . . 17 B2
Headland Rd TR26 . . . 17 B2
HEAMOOR 22 B3
Heamoor Prim Sch
 TR18 . . . . 22 B2
Hea Rd TR18 . . . . 22 C3
Heatherbell Gdns
 TR26 . . . . 17 B1
Heather Cl TR18 . . . . . 22 B3
Heather La TR27 . . . . . . 6 C3
Heather Way TR20 . . . 11 C1
Helca Dr TR26 . . . . . . 16 C3
Hellesvean **2** TR26 . . . 2 B3
Hellesvean Cl **3** TR26 . 2 B3
HELLESVEOR 2 B4

Helnoweth Cotts
 TR18 . . . . 23 C4
Helnoweth Gdns
 TR18 . . . . 23 C4
Helnoweth Hill TR18 . 23 C4
Hendras Ct TR26 . . . . 17 B2
Hendras Parc TR26 . . 17 A2
Hendra Vean TR26 . . . 17 B1
Henfor Cl **12** TR17 . . . 10 C2
Henfor Mews **6**
 TR17 . . . . 10 C2
Henfor Terr **13** TR17 . . 10 C2
Herland Hill TR27 . . . . 5 B1
HIGHER
 BOSCASWELL 12 C4
Higher Boskerris
 TR26 . . . . 17 A1
Higher Burrow Cl
 TR26 . . . . 16 A4
Higher Church St
 TR27 . . . . 19 A2
HIGHER DOWNS 11 C2
Higher Fore St TR17 . . 10 C2
Higher Green St
 TR18 . . . . 25 A1
Higher Gwavas Rd **3**
 TR18 . . . . 24 C1
Higher Lariggan
 TR18 . . . . 25 A4
Higher Lidden Rd
 TR18 . . . . 24 C3
Higher Peverell Rd
 TR18 . . . . 23 B3
Higher Stennack
 TR26 . . . . 14 A1
Higher Tregenna Rd
 TR26 . . . . 16 B3
Higher Trevithick
 TR27 . . . . 19 A1
Higher Trewidden Rd
 TR26 . . . . 16 B4
Highfields **19** TR18 . . 24 C2
HIGH LANES 19 A1
High Lanes TR27 . . . . 19 A1
High St
 Penzance TR18 . . . . . . 23 B1
 St Ives TR26 . . . . 14 B2
Hill Cl TR18 . . . . 22 B3
Hillcrest Rd TR27 . . . . 19 A2
Hillside TR19 . . . . 12 B3
Hillside Ct TR27 . . . . . . 5 A2
Hillside Parc TR20 . . . . 8 B4
Hillside Terr **22** TR18 . 24 C2
Hollies The TR27 . . . . . 20 B4
Hollow's Terr TR27 . . 19 B3
Holly Terr **9** TR18 . . 22 C3
Horsepool Rd TR27 . . . 5 C3
Humphry Davy La
 TR27 . . . . 19 A1
Humphry Davy Sch
 TR18 . . . . 23 B2

I

Island Rd **4** TR26 . . . .14 B2
Island Sq **8** TR26 . . . .14 B2
Ivy La TR18 . . . . .22 C1

J

Jack La TR18. . . . . . . .24 C2
Jack Stephens Est
TR18 . . . . .23 A2
Jamaica Pl **14** TR18. . .22 C3
Jamaica Terr **13**
TR18 . . . . .22 C3
Jelbert Way TR18 . . . . . . 9 B3
Jennings St TR18. . . . .23 B1
Jericho La TR27. . . . . .21 A1
John Ellis Ct TR27. . . . .18 C1
John's Cnr TR20 . . . . .11 C2
JOPPA. 21 B4
Joseph's La TR18. . . . .22 C4
Jubilee Bglws **20**
TR18 . . . . .24 C1
Jubilee Ct **15** TR26 . . . . 2 B3
Jubilee Poll TR18 . . . .25 C4

K

Karenza Ct TR26 . . . . .17 B2
Keigwen Pl TR19 . . . . .13 B3
Kelwyn Ct TR26 . . . . . .16 C2
Kenidjack Cl TR26. . . .17 B1
Kensa Way TR27. . . . . . .5 C3
Kenstella Rd TR18. . . .24 C2
Kenython La TR19 . . . .12 B2
Kernick Way TR27 . . . .19 B4
Kew Vean TR26. . . . . . .16 C3
King George V Memorial
Wlk TR27 . . . . .18 C2
Kings Rd TR17 . . . . . . .10 B2
King's Rd TR18. . . . . . .23 A1
Kittiwake Cl TR27 . . . . .7 A4
Kitts Ct **17** TR18 . . . . .23 B1
Knill Cl TR26 . . . . .16 C2

L

Lafrowda Cl TR19 . . . .12 A1
Lafrowda Terr TR19. . . .12 B1
Laity La TR26 . . . . .3 A1
Lancamshire La
TR20 . . . . .11 C2
Landeryon Gdns
TR18 . . . . .23 A1
Landithy TR20. . . . . . .22 A4
Lane Reddin Terr **21**
TR18 . . . . .24 C2
Langweath Gdns TR27 7 A4
Lannoweth Rd TR18 . .23 C2
Lansdowne TR26 . . . . .16 B4
Lansdowne Cl TR18 . .22 C1

Lansdowne Ct TR18 . .22 B1
Lansdowne Pl TR18 . .24 C4
Lansdowne Rd TR18 . .22 C1
Lanuthnoe Est TR27 . . . 7 B2
Laregan Hill TR18 . . . .24 C3
Lariggan Cres TR18 . . .25 A4
Lariggan Rd TR18 . . . .25 A4
Leat Rd TR19. . . . . . . .12 C4
LELANT. 3 C1
LELANT DOWNS. 6 C3
Lelant Mdws TR26. . . . . 3 C1
Lelant Saltings Sta
TR26 . . . . .7 A4
Lelant Sta TR26 . . . . . .3 C1
Lescudjack Cres
TR18 . . . . .23 C2
Lescudjack Rd TR18 . .23 B2
Lescudjack Terr
TR18 . . . . .23 C2
Lesingey La TR20. . . . . .8 A2
Leskinnick Pl **14**
TR18 . . . . .23 B2
Leskinnick St TR18 . . .23 C2
Leskinnick Terr TR18 . .23 B2
Lethlean Cl TR27 . . . . .19 A3
Lethlean La TR27 . . . . .19 A3
Lethlean Towans
TR27 . . . . .19 A4
Levant Cl TR19 . . . . . . .12 B3
Levant Mine & Beam
Engine* TR19 . . . . . . .12 A4
Levant Rd TR19 . . . . . .12 B3
Leys La TR17. . . . . .10 B2
Lidden Cl TR18 . . . . . . .24 C3
Lidden Cres TR18 . . . . .24 C3
Lidden Rd TR18 . . . . . .24 C3
Lifeboat Hill **32** TR26 . .14 B2
Little-in-sight **19**
TR26 . . . . .14 A1
Little La TR27 . . . . .19 B3
Little Mill La TR27. . . . .7 A3
Logans Ct TR26 . . . . . .17 A2
Loggans Cl TR27 . . . . .19 B4
Loggans Rd TR27. . . . .19 C4
Loggans Way TR27 . . .19 B4
Loggans Wlk TR27. . . .19 B4
Lomond Hall TR26. . . .17 A1
Long Barn The TR20 . . .6 C1
Long La
Ludgvan TR20 . . . . .10 A4
St Erth TR20, TR27. . . . . .7 A1
Long Lanes TR20 . . . . .11 C4
LONGROCK 9 C3
Longrock Bsns Pk
TR20 . . . . .9 C3
Longrock Ind Est
TR20 . . . . .9 C3
LONGSTONE 17 B1
Longstone Cl TR26 . . .17 B1
Longstone Hill TR26. . .17 B1
Love La
Hayle TR27. . . . . .19 B3
Mousehole TR19 . . . . . .13 B3
Penzance TR18 . . . . . . .24 C4

Love La continued
24 St Ives TR26. . . . . . .14 B2
Lowenac Cres TR27 . . .5 C3
Lower Boscaswell Parc
TR19 . . . . .12 B4
Lower Church St
TR27 . . . . .19 A2
Lower Green St TR18 .25 A1
Lower Gurnick Rd
TR18 . . . . .24 B3
Lower Peverell Rd
TR18 . . . . .23 B3
Low Lee Rd TR19 . . . . .13 C3
LUDGVAN. 10 A4
Ludgvan Prim Sch
TR20 . . . . .6 A1
Luke's La TR20 . . . . . . .11 C3
Lyn Terr **7** TR18. . . . . .24 C1
Lynwood Cotts **1**
TR19 . . . . .13 B3

M

Mabbots Ct TR18 . . . . .23 C2
Madison Terr TR27. . . .19 B3
Madison Vean TR27. . . .19 B3
MADRON 22 B4
Madron Rd TR18 . . . . .22 C3
Main St TR18. . . . . . . .22 C3
Malt House Ct TR27 . . .19 A2
Malt House Gdns **2**
TR18 . . . . .24 C2
Malthouse La TR17. . . .10 C2
Malt House The **3**
TR18 . . . . .24 C2
Manor Cl TR18 . . . . . . .23 A3
Manor Dr TR26. . . . . . .16 C3
Manor Farm Cl **7**
TR20 . . . . .11 B2
Manor Gdns TR27 . . . .20 A1
Manor Pl TR18 . . . . . . .23 A3
Manor Way TR18 . . . . .23 A3
MARAZION 10 B3
Marazion Mus*
TR17 . . . . .10 B2
Marazion Sch TR17. . . .10 C2
Marcwheal **6** TR19. . . .13 B3
Marine Terr **7** TR18 . .25 B4
Market Ct TR27 . . . . . .19 A2
Market Jew St TR18 . .23 B1
Market Pl
Marazion TR17. . . . . . . .10 B2
25 Penzance TR18. . . . .23 B1
33 St Ives TR26. . . . . . .14 B2
Market Sq
Hayle TR27. . . . . .19 A2
St Just TR19 . . . . .12 B1
Market St
Hayle TR27. . . . . .19 A2
St Just TR19 . . . . .12 B1
Market Strand **31**
TR26 . . . . .14 B2
Marsh La
Angarrack TR27. . . . . . .19 C3

Marsh La continued
Hayle TR27. . . . . .19 B3
Mead Hos The TR18 . .23 C4
Meadow Flats **27**
TR26 . . . . .14 B2
Meadowside Cl TR27 .20 A3
Meadow The **47**
TR26 . . . . .14 B2
Meadow View **8**
TR20 . . . . .11 B2
Meadow Villas **8**
TR18 . . . . .24 C1
Medrose Terr **21**
TR18 . . . . .23 B2
Melbourne Terr **17**
TR18 . . . . .22 C3
Mellanear Cl TR27. . . .20 B4
Mellanear Ct TR27 . . .20 B4
Mellanear Rd TR27 . . .20 B3
Melyn Cl TR27 . . . . . . .19 B4
Menhyr Dr TR26. . . . . .16 C2
Mennaye Ct TR18 . . . .25 A4
Mennaye Rd TR18 . . . .25 A4
Mews The **3** TR18 . . . .23 B2
Mexico La TR27 . . . . . .18 C3
Mexico Terr TR27. . . . .18 C4
Middle Stennack Cotts
13 TR26 . . . . .14 A1
Millet Cl TR17. . . . . . . .11 A2
Millfield TR18. . . . . .9 B3
Mill Hill TR27 . . . . .7 A4
Mill La **20** TR19. . . . . . .13 B3
Millpond Ave TR27 . . .20 B4
Mission The TR18 . . . .25 C4
Moonrakers TR26 . . . .17 A2
Moorland Cl TR19 . . . .12 B4
Morrab Pl **34** TR18. . . .23 B1
Morrab Rd TR18. . . . . .23 B1
Morrab Terr **35** TR18 .23 B1
Mount Folly TR27. . . . .18 C2
Mount Lidden TR18. . . .24 C1
Mount Pleasant
Hayle TR27. . . . . .18 C2
Lelant TR26 . . . . .7 A4
Newlyn TR18 . . . . .24 C4
39 St Ives TR26. . . . . . .14 B2
Mount Pleasant Gdns
TR27 . . . . .18 C2
Mount Pleasant Terr
TR19 . . . . .13 B3
Mount Prospect Terr
TR18 . . . . .24 C2
Mount Royal Cl TR18 .23 C2
Mounts Bay Rd TR18. .24 C4
Mount's Bay Sch
TR18 . . . . .22 B3
Mount St TR18 . . . . . . .23 B2
Mount View TR20. . . . . .8 A4
Mount View Cotts
TR20 . . . . .10 A4
Mount View Terr
5 Marazion TR17. . . . .10 C2
24 Newlyn TR18 . . . .24 C2
Mount Zion **52** TR26 . .14 B2

MOUSEHOLE 13 C3
Mousehole La TR19 . . 13 B3
Mousehole Prim Sch
TR19 . . . . 13 B3
Murray Villas TR19 . . . 12 A1
Mutton Hill TR27 . . . . . . 5 B3
Mythyon Ct **4** TR18 . . 22 C3

N

Nampara Cl TR26 . . . . . 17 B2
Nancealverne TR18. . . 23 A2
Nancealverne Specl Sch
TR20 . . . . 22 C2
Nancherrow Hill
TR19 . . . . 12 B1
Nancherrow Row
TR19 . . . . 12 B1
Nanjivey Pl **8** TR26 . . 14 A1
Nanjivey Terr **9**
TR26 . . . . 14 A1
Nanpusker Cl TR27 . . . 19 B2
Nanpusker Rd TR27 . . . 5 A1
Nanturras Parc TR20 . 11 C2
Nanturras Row TR20. . 11 B2
Navy Inn Ct **10** TR18 . . 24 C1
Nevada Pl **16** TR18. . . . 22 C3
Nevada St TR18 . . . . . . 22 C3
New Dairy La TR17 . . . 10 B3
NEW DOWNS 12 A1
NEWLYN. 25 A2
Newlyn Art Gall★
TR18 . . . . 24 C3
Newlyn Prim Sch
TR18 . . . . 24 C3
New Rd
Newlyn TR18 . . . . 24 C3
St Hilary TR20 . . . . 11 C3
St Just TR19 . . . . 12 B1
New St TR18 . . . . 23 B1
Newtown La TR17,
TR20 . . . . 10 A4
New Town La TR18. . . . 23 B1
Nicholas Parc **3**
TR18 . . . . 22 C3
NINNIS BRIDGE 6 A3
No Go By Hill TR19 . . . 12 B2
North Cliff **12** TR19 . . 13 B3
North Cnr **1** TR18. . . . 24 C2
North Orchard Ct **1**
TR20 . . . . 11 B2
North Par TR18 . . . . . . 23 B1
North Pl **15** TR26 . . . . 14 B2
North Quay TR27 . . . . . 18 B2
North Rd TR20 . . . . 11 B2
North Row TR19. . . . . . 12 B1
North St
Marazion TR17. . . . . . . 10 B2
14 Mousehole TR19. . . 13 B3
North Terr
2 Penzance TR18. . . . 25 B4
12 St Ives TR26. . . . . . 14 B1
Nut La TR27. . . . . 7 A4

O

Oates Rd TR17 . . . . 10 C2
Ocean View Terr
TR26 . . . . 14 A2
Old Bakehouse Flats
The TR18 . . . . 23 C2
Old Brewery Yd **4**
TR18 . . . . 23 B1
Old Butchers Shop The
TR20 . . . . 6 A1
Old Church The
TR18 . . . . 25 A4
Old Foundry Cl TR19. . 12 B1
Old Paul Hill TR18. . . . 24 C2
Old Smithy Cl **4**
TR17 . . . . 10 C2
Old Sta La TR17 . . . . . . 10 A3
Old Vicarage Gate
TR27 . . . . 20 A1
Orange La TR26 . . . . . . 14 A2
Orchard Ct TR18 . . . . . 22 C1
Orchard Ho **11** TR18 . . 24 C2
Orchard Pl **10** TR18. . . 24 C2
Orchard Terr **20**
TR18 . . . . 24 C2
Orchard The TR27 . . . . . 7 A3
Orchard Way **6**
TR20 . . . . 11 B2

P

Packet La TR20. . . . . . . 11 C2
Padnover Terr **22**
TR26 . . . . 14 B1
Pannier La TR26. . . . . . 16 C2
Parade Hill TR19 . . . . . 13 C3
Parade Pass **29** TR18 . 23 B1
Parade St TR18 . . . . . . 23 B1
Parade The TR19 . . . . . 13 C3
Paradise Park & The
World Parrot Trust★
TR27 . . . . 20 A4
Parc-Abnac TR20 . . . . . 8 B4
Parc-an-Creet TR26. . . 2 B4
Parc-an-Dix La TR27 18 C3
Parc-an-Forth **6**
TR26 . . . . 2 B3
Parc an Gate TR19. . . . 13 B3
Parc-an-Stamps **4**
TR26 . . . . 2 B3
Parc an Yorth TR19 . . . 12 B3
Parc Bean Terr TR26. . 14 A2
Parc Letta TR18 . . . . . . 22 C3
Parc Mellan TR18 . . . . 23 A3
Parc Owles TR26 . . . . . . 2 B3
Parc Shady TR26 . . . . . . 6 B2
Parc Terr **19** TR18. . . . 24 C1
Parc Villas **17** TR18 . . 24 C1
Parc Wartha Ave
TR18 . . . . 23 A2
Parc Wartha Cres
TR18 . . . . 23 A2

Park an Gonwyn
TR26 . . . . 17 B2
Park-an-Pyth TR19 . . 12 C4
Park Ave TR26 . . . . 14 B1
Park Cnr TR18 . . . . 23 B1
Park Ct **28** TR18 . . . . . 23 B1
Park Lowen TR26. . . . . 16 C2
Park Rd **18** TR18. . . . . . 24 C1
Parkryn Rd **4** TR19 . . 13 B3
Pathway Fields The
TR27 . . . . 18 C1
PAUL 13 B4
Pearce's La **12** TR26 . . 14 A1
Pednandrea TR19 . . . . 12 A1
Penalverne Ave TR18 23 A1
Penalverne Cres
TR18 . . . . 23 A1
Penalverne Dr TR18 . . 23 A1
Penalverne Pl TR18 . . 23 A1
Penameyne Ct **5**
TR26 . . . . 14 B2
Pen-an-Gwel TR26. . . 16 A4
Penare Gdns **2** TR18 23 B2
Penare Rd TR18 . . . . . . 23 B2
Penare Terr TR18. . . . . 23 B2
Penarwyn Cres TR18 . 22 B3
PENBEAGLE 16 A4
Penbeagle Cl **17** TR26 . 2 B3
Penbeagle Cres **8**
TR26 . . . . 2 B3
Penbeagle Ind Est
TR26 . . . . 2 B3
Penbeagle La TR26. . . . 2 B3
Penbeagle Terr **7**
TR26 . . . . 2 B3
Penbeagle Way TR26 .16 A4
PENBERTH. 13 A3
Penberthy Cross
TR27 . . . . 11 C4
Penbrea Rd TR18. . . . . 23 B3
Pendarves Flats
TR18 . . . . 23 A2
Pendarves Rd TR18. . . 23 A2
PENDEEN. 12 C4
Pendeen Prim Sch
TR19 . . . . 12 C4
Pendennis Cl TR18 . . . 23 B3
Pendennis Pl TR18 . . . 23 C3
Pendennis Rd TR18. . . 23 B3
Pendola Wlk TR26. . . . 14 B1
Pendrea Cl TR18 . . . . . 23 C3
Pendrea Pl TR18 . . . . . 23 C3
Pendrea Rd TR18. . . . . 23 C3
Pengwel **16** TR18. . . . . 24 C2
Penkernick Cl TR18 . 24 B1
Penlee House Gall &
Mus★ TR18. . . . . 23 B1
Penlee Manor Dr
TR18 . . . . 25 B4
Penlee St TR18 . . . . . . 23 B2
Penlee View Terr **3**
TR18 . . . . 25 B4
Penmare Cl TR27. . . . . 19 B3
Penmare Ct TR27. . . . . 19 B3

Penmare Terr TR27 . . . 19 B3
Penmere Cl TR18. . . . . 23 B3
Penmere Pl TR18. . . . . 23 B3
Penmere Rd TR18 . . . . 23 B3
Penpol Ave TR27 . . . . . 18 C1
Penpol Prim Sch
TR27 . . . . 18 C1
Penpol Rd TR27 . . . . . . 18 B1
Penpol Terr TR27 . . . . 18 B1
Penpol Vean TR27 . . . . 18 C1
Penpons Cl TR18 . . . . . 24 C4
Pen Porth Ave TR26 . . . 2 B4
Penrose Ct TR18 . . . . . 23 C2
Penrose Terr TR18. . . . 23 C2
Pensans Com Prim Sch
TR18 . . . . 23 A2
Pentowan Ct TR26. . . . 17 B2
Pentowan Gdns TR27 19 B4
Pentowan Rd TR27 . . . 19 B4
Pentreath Cl TR18 . . . . 23 A3
Penwith Bsns Ctr
TR20 . . . . 9 C3
Penwith Cl TR26 . . . . . 16 A4
Penwith Coll TR18 . . . 23 A2
Penwithian Cl TR27 . . 19 B2
Penwith Rd TR26. . . . . 16 A4
Penwith St **11** TR18. . . 23 B2
PENZANCE 23 C1
Penzance L Ctr TR18 .23 A2
Penzance School of Art
TR18 . . . . 23 B1
Penzance Sta TR18. . . 23 C2
Perran Crossroads
TR20 . . . . 11 B2
PERRAN DOWNS 11 B2
PERRANUTHNOE 11 A1
Peters Row TR19. . . . . 12 C4
Petes Pl **24** TR26 . . . . 14 B1
Peverell Rd TR18. . . . . 23 B3
Philgray Cl TR27 . . . . . 19 B3
PHILLACK 19 A3
Phillack Hill TR27 . . . . 19 A3
Piala Pl TR27 . . . . 19 B3
Piazza **14** TR26 . . . . . . 14 B2
Pilchard Works The★
TR18 . . . . 24 C3
Pine Rd TR18 . . . . 24 B4
Pintail Ave TR27. . . . . . 7 A4
Plantation La TR27 . . . 18 B1
Pleasant Pl **18** TR18 . . 22 C3
Poldhu Cl TR26 . . . . . . 17 A1
Polgarth TR18 . . . . 24 B3
Polgarth Cl TR26 . . . . . 17 A1
Polglaze TR18 . . . . 23 A3
Polgoon Cl TR18 . . . . . 22 C1
Polmeere Ho TR18 . . . 23 B3
Polmeere Rd TR18 . . . 23 B3
Polmennor Dr TR26 . . 17 A1
Polmennor Rd TR18 . . 22 C4
Polmeor Cl TR26 . . . . . 17 A1
Polmor Rd TR20. . . . . . . 6 A1
POLPEOR. 6 A4

Polruan Cl TR26 . . . . **3** A1
Poltair Cl TR18 . . . . . . **22** C3
Poltair Hospl TR20 . . **22** B4
Poltair Terr **7** TR18 . . **22** C3
Poltreen Cl TR26 . . . . . **17** A1
Polvelyn Parc TR27 . . . **19** B3
Polventon Cl TR18 . . . **22** C3
Polweath Cl TR18 . . . . **23** B3
Polweath Rd TR18 . . . **23** B3
Polwithen Ct TR26 . . . **16** C2
Polwithen Dr TR26 . . . **16** C1
Polwithen Gdns
  TR26 . . . . **16** C1
Polwithen Rd TR18 . . . **23** A1
Polwyn Cl TR18 . . . . . . **22** B3
Pond Wlk TR27 . . . . . . **19** A3
Poniou La TR20 . . . . **9** C3
Poniou Rd TR20 . . . . **9** C3
Poniou Way TR20 . . . . . **9** C3
Ponsandane Farm Mews
  TR18 . . . . **23** C3
Pool's Ct TR27 . . . . **19** A2
Pordenack Cl TR26 . . . **17** B2
Porthcollum La TR27 . . **7** C2
Portherras Cross
  TR19 . . . . **12** C4
Portherras Terr
  TR19 . . . . **12** C4
Portherras Villas
  TR19 . . . . **12** C4
Porthgwidden Studios
  TR26 . . . . **14** C2
Porthia Cl TR26 . . . . . . **16** A4
Porthia Cres TR26 . . . . **16** A4
Porthia Rd **12** TR26 . . . . **2** B3
Porthmeor Ct **51**
  TR26 . . . . **14** B2
Porthmeor Hill TR26 . . **14** A2
Porthmeor Rd **6**
  TR26 . . . . **14** B2
Porthmeor Sq **21**
  TR26 . . . . **14** B2
Porthmeor Studios **50**
  TR26 . . . . **14** B2
Porthminster Terr **23**
  TR26 . . . . **14** B1
Porthrepta Rd TR26 . . **17** B1
Portland Pl **23** TR19 . . **13** B3
Posses La TR18 . . . . **9** B3
Praed Pl TR26 . . . . **3** C1
Praed's La TR17 . . . . . . **10** C2
Praze-an-Creet TR26 . . **2** B4
Prevenna Rd **2** TR19 **13** B3
Primrose Cl **9** TR20 . . **11** B2
Primrose Ct TR26 . . . . **16** B4
Primrose Hill TR20 . . . **11** B2
Primrose La **4** TR20 . . **11** B2
Primrose Terr TR18 . . . **25** A1
Primrose Valley
  TR26 . . . . **16** C4
Princess Ct **12** TR18 . . **23** B1
Princes St TR18 . . . . . . **23** B1

Priors Cl **10** TR26 . . . . . . **2** B3
Prospect Cl TR27 . . . . . **19** A2
Prospect Pl
  Hayle TR27 . . . . **19** A2
  25 Penzance TR18 . . . . **23** B2
Prout's La TR27 . . . . **5** B3
Provis Rd TR18 . . . . **24** C4
PZ Gall* TR18 . . . . **25** C4

Q

Quarry Gdns TR18 . . . . **23** A1
Quarry Hill TR18 . . . . . . **9** B4
Quay St
  11 Mousehole TR19 . . **13** B3
  Penzance TR18 . . . . **25** C4
  St Ives TR26 . . . . **14** C2
Quay The TR18 . . . . **23** C1
Queen's Ct **6** TR18 . . **25** B4
Queen's Sq **24** TR18 . . **23** B1
Queen St
  Goldsithney TR20 . . . . . **11** B2
  Penzance TR18 . . . . **23** B1
  St Just TR19 . . . . **12** A1
Queen's Way
  2 Goldsithney
  TR20 . . . . **11** B2
  Hayle TR27 . . . . **18** C1
Quillet Rd TR18 . . . . . . **24** B3

R

Raginnis Hill **25** TR19 **13** B3
Redfern Ct **2** TR26 . . . **14** B1
Redinnick Gdns **4**
  TR18 . . . . **25** B4
Redinnick Pl TR18 . . . . **25** A4
Redinnick Terr **1**
  TR18 . . . . **25** B4
Red La TR20 . . . . **11** C2
Reens Cres TR18 . . . . . **23** A3
Reens Rd TR18 . . . . **22** C3
Regent Bldgs **36**
  TR18 . . . . **23** B1
Regent Sq **21** TR18 . . **23** B1
Regent Terr
  Penzance TR18 . . . . **25** B4
  St Just TR19 . . . . **12** A1
Rescorla Ct TR27 . . . . . **18** C1
Restormel Rd TR18 . . . **24** C3
Retallack Gdns **3**
  TR20 . . . . **11** B2
Richmond Pl **40** TR26 **14** B2
Richmond St
  Heamoor TR18 . . . . **22** C3
  Penzance TR18 . . . . **23** B2
Richmond Way TR26 . . **17** A1
Ridgeo Mill TR18 . . . . . **23** C4
Ridgevale Cl TR18 . . . . **23** C4
Ridgevale La TR18 . . . . **23** C4
Riverside
  Angarrack TR27 . . . . **5** A1
  Lelant TR26 . . . . **3** C1
Riverside Mews TR27 . . **5** A2

Riviera Apartments
  TR26 . . . . **17** A2
RIVIERE TOWANS **18** B3
Riviere Towans TR27 . . **18** B3
Roach's Ct TR26 . . . . . . **17** B1
Rock Close Ho TR27 . . **20** A1
Rock Rd TR18 . . . . **24** C3
Rock Terr TR18 . . . . **22** C3
Roma Ct TR27 . . . . **18** B1
Ropewalk The TR18 . . **24** C4
Rope Wlk The **3**
  TR26 . . . . **14** B2
Roscadghill Parc **1**
  TR18 . . . . **22** C3
Roscadghill Rd TR18 . . **22** C2
ROSE-AN-GROUSE . . . **6** C3
Rosehill TR17 . . . . **10** B2
Rosehill Gdns TR18 . . . **22** B2
Rosehill Mdw TR18 . . . **22** B2
Rose La **23** TR26 . . . . . **14** B2
Rosemorran **23** TR26 . **14** B1
Rose Terr **22** TR18 . . . **23** B2
Rosevale TR18 . . . . **25** A4
Rosevean Rd TR18 . . . . **23** B2
Rosevean Terr TR18 . . **23** B2
Rosewall Cotts **16**
  TR26 . . . . **14** A1
Rosewall Terr **17**
  TR26 . . . . **14** A1
Rosewithian Cl TR27 . . **5** C3
Roskilly Cotts TR19 . . . **13** B4
Ros Lyn TR26 . . . . **16** C1
Rosparvah Gdns
  TR18 . . . . **22** C3
Rospeath La TR20 . . . . **10** C4
ROSUDGEON **11** C1

S

Sail Loft Flats **2**
  TR26 . . . . **14** B2
St Andrew's St **1**
  TR26 . . . . **14** B1
St Annes Ct TR26 . . . . . **3** C1
St Anta Rd TR26 . . . . . . **17** B1
St Aubyns TR20 . . . . . . **11** B2
St Clare Flats TR18 . . . **23** A2
St Clare St TR18 . . . . . . **23** A2
St Clements Terr **26**
  TR19 . . . . **13** B3
St Dominic St **8**
  TR18 . . . . **23** B2
St Eia St TR26 . . . . **14** C2
St Elwyns Rise TR27 . . **18** B2
ST ERTH **20** A1
St Erth Com Prim Sch
  TR27 . . . . **20** A1
St Erth Hill TR27 . . . . . . **7** B2
St Erth Ind Est TR27 . . **7** A3
ST ERTH PRAZE **21** C1
St Erth Sta TR27 . . . . . . **7** A3
St Francis St **5** TR18 **23** B2
St George's Rd TR27 . . **18** C1
St Golder Rd TR18 . . . . **24** B3

St Henry St **4** TR18 . . **23** B2
ST HILARY **11** B3
St Hilary Prim Sch
  TR20 . . . . **11** C3
St Ia Sch TR26 . . . . **17** A1
ST IVES **14** C2
St Ives Jun & Inf Schs
  TR26 . . . . **14** A1
St Ives L Ctr TR26 . . . . **14** A1
St Ives Mus* TR26 . . . **14** C2
St Ives Mushroom Farm
  TR26 . . . . **2** B3
St Ives Rd
  Carbis Bay TR26 . . . . . . **17** A1
  Pendeen TR19 . . . . **12** C4
St Ives Sch TR26 . . . . . **16** B3
St Ives Sta TR26 . . . . . . **14** B1
St James' St TR18 . . . . **23** B1
St Johns Ct **7** TR18 . . **23** B1
St John's Ct TR27 . . . . . **19** A2
St John's St TR27 . . . . . **19** A2
St John's Terr TR19 . . . **12** C4
St Johns Wlk TR26 . . . . **2** B4
ST JUST **12** A1
St Just Prim Sch
  TR19 . . . . **12** A1
St Levan Cl **8** TR17 . . **10** C4
St Levan Rd **7** TR17 . . **10** C4
St Madderns CE Sch
  TR20 . . . . **22** A4
St Mary's CE Prim Sch
  TR18 . . . . **25** B4
St Mary's RC Sch
  TR18 . . . . **23** B3
St Mary's St TR18 . . . . **23** B2
St Mary's Terr TR18 . . **23** B1
St Michael's Cl TR27 . . **20** B4
St Michael's Cotts **11**
  TR18 . . . . **23** B1
St Michaels Ct **18**
  TR18 . . . . **23** B1
St Michael's Hospl
  TR27 . . . . **20** B4
St Michael's Mount*
  TR17 . . . . **10** B1
St Michael's St TR18 . . **23** B2
St Michael's Terr
  TR18 . . . . **23** A2
St Nicholas Cl TR27 . . . **5** A3
St Nicholas Ct **1**
  TR26 . . . . **14** B2
St Peter's Hill TR18 . . . **24** C1
St Peters St **16** TR26 . **14** B2
St Petry TR20 . . . . **11** B2
St Philip St **7** TR18 . . **23** B2
St Pirans Ct **13** TR18 . **23** B1
St Piran's Sch TR27 . . . **20** B4
St Pirans Way TR20 . . . **11** A1
St Pol de Leon View
  TR19 . . . . **13** B4
St Uny CE Sch TR26 . . **17** A1
St Uny Cl TR26 . . . . **7** A4
St Warren St **6**
  TR18 . . . . **23** B2

Saltings Cl TR26 . . . . 7 A4
Saltings Reach TR26. . . 7 A4
Saltings The TR26 . . . . . 3 C1
Saltponds 27 TR19 . . . 13 B3
Sampson's Ct TR27. . . . 5 B3
Sandows La 15 TR26. . 14 A1
Sandyacres TR27. . . . . . 4 C3
Sandy Acres TR27 . . . . 19 B4
School La
Gulval TR18 . . . . 9 B3
Marazion TR17. . . . . . . 10 C2
St Erth TR27. . . . . 20 A1
St Hilary TR20 . . . . 11 C3
Sea La TR27. . . . . 19 A2
Sea Urchin TR26 . . . . . 17 B2
Sea View Pl TR26. . . . . 14 C2
Sea View Terr
6 Newlyn TR18 . . . . . . 24 C1
20 St Ives TR26. . . . . . 14 B1
Sheila's Ct TR26. . . . . . 17 A1
Shop Hill 3 TR17 . . . . 10 C2
Simpsons Ct 30 TR18 . 23 B1
Skidden Hill 18 TR26 . 14 B1
Sona Merg Cl TR18 . . 22 C3
South Cliff 18 TR19 . . 13 B3
Southfields Pl 3
TR26 . . . . 14 A1
South Par 33 TR18. . . 23 B1
South Pl TR19. . . . . . . 12 A1
South Place Folly 5
TR18 . . . . 25 B4
South Place Gdns
TR19 . . . . 12 A1
South Rd TR20 . . . . 11 B2
South Terr 12 TR18 . . 25 B4
Southview Terr 8
TR19 . . . . 13 B3
Spernen Cl TR26 . . . . . 16 C2
Springfield Cl TR27. . . 19 A3
Springfield Rd TR20 . . 11 B2
Square The
Marazion TR17. . . . . . . 10 B2
Pendeen TR19 . . . . 12 C4
Stable Hobba Ind Est
TR18 . . . . 24 B3
Stanford Cl 5 TR18 . . 23 A1
Stanford Terr TR18 . . . 23 A1
START 7 A4
Station App TR27. . . . . 7 A3
Station Hill
Hayle TR27. . . . . 18 B1
Lelant TR26 . . . . 3 C1
Station Rd TR18 . . . . . 23 C2
Steamers Hill TR27. . . . 5 A2
Steamers Mdw TR27. . . 5 A2
Steeple Cl TR26 . . . . . 16 B3
Steeple La TR26 . . . . . 16 B3
Steeple View Ct
TR26 . . . . 16 C1
Steeple Woodland
Nature Reserve★
TR26 . . . . 16 B3
Stennack Gdns 14
TR26 . . . . 14 A1

Stennack Parc TR19 . . 12 B3
Stennack The TR26 . . . 14 B1
Steppy Downs Rd
TR27 . . . . 7 C2
Stones Ct 30 TR26 . . . 14 B1
Strand TR18 . . . . 24 C2
Strawberry La
Hayle TR27. . . . . 21 A4
Lelant TR26 . . . . 3 C1
TR26 . . . . 14 B1
Street-an-Garrow 17
TR26 . . . . 14 B1
Street-an-Pol 3
TR26 . . . . 14 B1
Strickland Cotts 6
TR18 . . . . 24 C2
Stringers Hill TR20 . . . . 8 A2
Sunny Cnr TR20 . . . . . . 11 C2
Sunny Terr TR18. . . . . . 24 B2
Sylverton Pl 12 TR18. . 22 C3

T

Talland Ct 29 TR26. . . 14 B1
Talland Rd TR26. . . . . . 14 B1
Talveneth TR19 . . . . . . 12 C4
Taroveor Rd TR18 . . . . 23 B2
Taroveor Terr 3
TR18 . . . . 23 B1
Tate St Ives (Gall)★
TR26 . . . . 14 B2
Teetotal St TR26 . . . . . 14 C2
Telcarne TR27 . . . . 5 B3
Tencreek Ave TR18 . . . 23 B1
Terrace The TR26. . . . . 14 B1
Teyla Tor Rd TR26 . . . . 17 A1
Thornberry Terr
TR18 . . . . 23 C2
Tinners Way 16 TR26 . . 2 B3
TOLCARNE. 24 C3
Tolcarne Terr TR18 . . . 24 C3
Tolpedn Flats TR26. . . 17 B2
Tolroy Rd TR27 . . . . 21 A1
Toltuff Cres TR18. . . . . 24 C4
Toltuff Rd TR18 . . . . . . 24 C4
Tolver Pl TR18 . . . . 23 B2
Tolver Rd TR18 . . . . 23 B2
Tolverth Terr TR20. . . . . 9 C3
Tolview Terr TR27 . . . . 20 B4
Towednack Rd TR26 . . . 2 B3
Trafalar Fields TR20 . . . 8 B4
Trafalgar Ct TR18 . . . . 23 C2
Trannack Terr TR18. . . 23 B3
Trease TR19. . . . . 12 C4
Treassowe Rd TR18. . . 23 B2
Treban Rd TR18 . . . . . . 24 C4
TREBARVAH 11 B1
Trebarvah La TR20 . . . 11 B1
Tredarvah Dr TR18 . . . 22 C1
Tredarvah Rd TR18 . . . 22 C1
TREDAVOE. 24 A2
Tredavoe La TR18 . . . . 24 B1
Tredrea La TR27. . . . . . . 7 A3
Treeve La TR27. . . . . 5 A3

Treeve Lane Ind Est
TR27 . . . . 5 A3
Tregarthen 2 TR26. . . 14 A1
Tregarth Pl TR18 . . . . . 24 C4
Tregassack Rd TR20 . . . 9 C4
Tregender La TR20 . . . . 6 A1
Tregender Rd TR20. . . . 6 A1
Tregenna Hill 16
TR26 . . . . 14 B1
Tregenna Parc TR26 . . 16 C3
Tregenna Pl 4 TR26. . 14 B1
Tregenna Terr TR26. . . 14 B1
TREGESEAL. 12 B2
Tregeseal Hill TR19. . . 12 B2
Tregeseal Row TR19. . 12 B1
Tregeseal Terr TR19 . . 12 B1
Treggodick Cotts
TR20 . . . . 22 A4
Tregie TR18. . . . . 24 B3
Treglyn Cl TR18 . . . . . . 24 B1
Tregoddick Cl TR20. . . . 8 B4
Tregos Rd TR26 . . . . . . 16 C2
Tregurtha Farm Cotts
TR17 . . . . 11 A3
Tregurtha View TR20. . 11 B2
Tregwary Rd TR26 . . . 14 A1
Trehayes Mdw TR27 . . . 7 A3
Trehayes Parc TR27 . . 19 B3
Trehurst TR18. . . . . 25 A4
Trelawney Ave TR26 . . 14 A1
Trelawney Est TR20. . . 22 A4
Trelawney Pl TR27. . . . 18 C2
Trelawney Rd TR26. . . 14 A1
Trelawney Way TR27. . 18 C2
Trelee Cl TR27 . . . . 19 B3
Trelissick Fields
TR27 . . . . 20 B3
Trelissick Rd TR27. . . . 20 B3
Treloweth Cl TR27. . . . . 7 A3
Treloweth La TR27. . . . . 7 A3
Treloyhan Cl TR26 . . . 16 C3
Treloyhan Park Rd
TR26 . . . . 16 C3
TRELYON. 16 B3
Trelyon Ave TR26. . . . . 16 C4
Tremaine Cl TR18 . . . . 22 C3
Tremar Rd TR26 . . . . . . 2 B4
Tremeadow Terr
TR27 . . . . 20 B4
Tremellin La TR27. . . . . 7 B2
Tremenheere Rd
TR18 . . . . 23 B2
TREMETHICK CROSS . 8 A2
Tremorva TR27. . . . . . . 18 C2
Trenawin La TR27 . . . . . 5 C2
TRENCROM 6 A4
Trencrom La TR26 . . . 17 A1
Trencrom Row TR20. . . 6 A4
Trendeal Gdns 1
TR18 . . . . 23 B1
Trendreath Cl TR26. . . . 7 A4
TRENEERE. 23 B3
Treneere La TR18. . . . . 23 A3
Treneere Rd TR18 . . . . 23 A2

Sal – Tre   33

Treneglos Terr
Gulval TR18 . . . . 9 B3
Newlyn TR18 . . . . 24 C3
Trengwainton Gdns★
TR20 . . . . 8 A3
Trenhayle La TR27. . . . 20 B2
Trenoweth Cres
TR18 . . . . 24 B4
Trenoweth Rd TR18. . . 22 B1
Trenwith La TR26. . . . . 16 A4
Trenwith Pl 14 TR26 . 14 B1
Trenwith Sq TR26 . . . . 14 A1
Trenwith Terr 11
TR26 . . . . 14 B1
Trerew Rd TR18 . . . . . . 24 C1
Trerice Pl TR26. . . . . . . 14 A1
Trerice Rd 6 TR26 . . . 14 A1
Trescoe Rd TR20 . . . . . . 9 C3
Trescowe Rd TR20. . . . 11 C2
Tresdale Parc TR27. . . . 5 B3
Tretorvic TR18 . . . . 22 C4
Trevale TR18. . . . . 22 C1
TREVARNON 5 B3
Trevarnon Rd TR27 . . . 5 B3
Trevarnon La TR27 . . . . 5 B3
Trevarrack Cl TR18 . . . 23 C4
Trevarrack La TR18. . . 23 C4
Trevarrack Pl TR18 . . . 23 C4
Trevarrack Rd TR18. . . 23 C4
Trevarrack Row TR18. . 9 B3
Trevarrick Ct TR26 . . . 14 B1
Trevarthian Ho TR17. . 10 B2
Trevassack Ct TR27. . . 19 A2
Trevassack Hill TR27. . 19 B2
Trevassack Parc
TR27 . . . . 19 B2
Trevean Gdns 3
TR18 . . . . 23 A1
Trevean La TR20. . . . . . 11 C1
Trevean Rd TR18 . . . . . 23 A1
Trevean Way TR20. . . . 11 C1
Treveglos TR27. . . . . . . 18 B2
Trevelyan Cl 10 TR20 . 11 B2
Trevelyan Way 5
TR20 . . . . 11 B2
Trevena Cl TR18. . . . . . 24 C4
Trevena Rd TR18 . . . . . 24 C4
Treveneth Cres TR18 . 24 C1
Treveneth Pl 1
TR18 . . . . 24 C1
Trevenner La TR17 . . . 10 C2
Trevenner Sq TR17 . . . 10 C2
Treverbyn Rd TR26 . . . 14 A1
Trevere Cl TR27 . . . . 5 A3
TREVETHOE 6 C4
Trevithick Cres TR27. . 19 A1
Trevoarn TR27 . . . . 18 B1
Trewartha Cl TR26. . . . 17 A1
Trewartha Est TR26. . . 17 A1
Trewartha Flats
TR26 . . . . 17 A1

Trewartha Terr **12**
TR18 . . . . .23 B2
Trewarveneth Farm
Cotts TR18 . . . . .13 B4
Trewarveneth St
TR18 . . . . .24 C2
Trewavas Rd TR18 . . . .24 C1
Treweath Rd TR18 . . . .23 A3
Treweeks Rd TR19 . . . .12 C4
TREWELLARD 12 B3
Trewellard Hill TR19 . .12 C3
Trewellard Ind Est
TR19 . . . . .12 B3
Trewellard Rd TR19 . . .12 B3
Trewhella La TR20 . . . .11 C4
Trewidden Gdn★
TR20 . . . . .8 A1
Trewidden Rd TR26 . . .14 B1
Trewince Terr **2**
TR18 . . . . .24 C1
Trewinnard La TR27 . . . .7 A2
Trewithen Rd TR18 . . .23 A1
Treworvenneth Dr **9**
TR17 . . . . .10 C2
Trewyn Flats **41**
TR26 . . . . .14 B2
Trezela Rd TR18 . . . . . .23 A2
Trunglemoor Cotts
TR19 . . . . .13 B4
Trungle Parc TR19 . . . .13 B4
Trungle Terr TR19 . . . .13 B4
TRUTHWALL
Marazion 11 A4
St Just 12 A2
Truthwall La TR19 . . . .12 B2
Tryhornek TR26 . . . . . . .3 B1
TRYTHOGGA 23 C4
Trythogga Hill TR18 . .23 C4
Trythogga Rd TR18 . . .23 C4
Turnpike Hill **2**
TR17 . . . . .10 C2

Turnpike Rd
Connor Downs TR27 . . . .5 B3
Marazion TR17 . . . . .10 C2
Turnpike The TR19 . . . .12 B1
Tyringham Pl TR26 . . . .3 C1
Tyringham Rd TR26 . . . .3 C1
Tyringham Row TR26 . .3 C1

U

Umfulla Pl **13** TR26 . . .14 B1
Under Chapel Yd
TR18 . . . . .25 C4
Undercliff TR27 . . . . . .19 A3
Union St **27** TR18 . . . . .23 B1
UPTON TOWANS 4 C3
Upton Twrs Nature
Reserve★ TR27 . . . . . . .4 C3

V

Valley Rd TR26 . . . . . . .16 C2
Varfell La TR20 . . . . . . .10 A4
Vellanhoggan Mews
TR18 . . . . .9 B3
Vellan Parc Ave TR27 . .5 A2
Vellan Vrane TR27 . . . . .5 A2
Ventnor Terr TR26 . . . .14 A2
Venton East Sq TR19 . .12 B1
VENTONLEAGUE 19 C3
Ventonleague Hill
TR27 . . . . .19 B3
Ventonleague Row
TR27 . . . . .19 B3
Venton Rd TR26 . . . . . .16 C3
Venton Vision Rise
TR26 . . . . .2 B4
Viaduct Hill TR27 . . . . .19 B2
Vicarage La TR26 . . . . . .3 C1
Victoria Ct **15** TR18 . . .23 B2
Victoria Mews **17**
TR18 . . . . 23 B2
Victoria Pl

Penzance TR18 . . . . .23 B1
12 St Ives TR26 . . . . . . .14 B2
Victoria Rd **11** TR26 . . .14 B2
Victoria Row TR19 . . . .12 A1
Victoria Sq **16** TR18 . . .23 B2
Villa Marina TR17 . . . .10 B2
Vingoe's La TR20 . . . . . .8 B4
Virgin Hill TR17 . . . . . .10 C3
Virgin Pl **16** TR19 . . . .13 B3
Virgin St **26** TR26 . . . . .14 B2
Vounder Glaze TR19 . .12 A1
Voundervour La **20**
TR18 . . . . .23 B1

W

Warren TR26 . . . . .14 B1
Water La TR27 . . . . .20 B3
Weethes Cotts **6**
TR18 . . . . .23 A1
Wellington Pl TR18 . . .23 A1
Well La TR20 . . . . .11 C2
Wesley Pl
5 Newlyn TR18 . . . . . .24 C2
7 St Ives TR26 . . . . . . .14 B1
Wesley St **11** TR18 . . . .22 C3
West Cornwall Hospl
TR18 . . . . .23 A2
West End
Goldsithney TR20 . . . . . .11 B2
Marazion TR17 . . . . .10 B2
Western Promenade Rd
TR18 . . . . .25 B4
West Pl
45 St Ives TR26 . . . . . . .14 B2
St Just TR19 . . . . .12 A1
West Terr
Hayle TR27 . . . . .18 B2
Newlyn TR18 . . . . .24 C3
Westward Rd TR26 . . .14 A2
Wharf Rd
Penzance TR18 . . . . . .23 C1
St Ives TR26 . . . . .14 B2

Wharfside **8** TR18 . . .23 B1
Wharfside Sh Ctr
TR18 . . . . .23 C1
Wharfside Village **9**
TR18 . . . . .23 B1
22 Mousehole TR19 . . .13 B3
St Ives TR26 . . . . .14 B2
WHEAL ALFRED 21 C4
Wheal Alfred Rd
TR27 . . . . .19 C1
Wheal-an-Wens
TR17 . . . . .10 C2
Wheal Dream TR26 . . .14 C2
Wheal Margery TR26 .16 C3
Wheal Speed Rd
TR26 . . . . .16 C2
Wheal Venture Rd
TR26 . . . . .16 C3
Wheal Virgin Ho TR26 . .2 B3
Wheal Whidden
TR26 . . . . .16 C2
Wheel Ayr Terr TR26 . .14 A2
WHERRY TOWN 25 A4
WHITECROSS 6 B2
White House Cl TR26 .16 C2
Widgeon Way TR27 . . . .7 A4
Willowfield TR18 . . . . .22 C1
Wills La **53** TR26 . . . . . .14 B2
Windsor Hill **8** TR26 .14 B1
Windsor Pl **28** TR18 . . .23 B2
Windsor Terr
Penzance TR18 . . . . . . .23 A2
4 St Ives TR26 . . . . . . .14 A1
Wolcocke Cl TR17 . . . .11 C4

Y

York St TR18 . . . . .23 A2

List of numbered locations

In some busy areas of the maps it is not always possible to show the name of every place.

Where not all names will fit, some smaller places are shown by a number. If you wish to find out the name associated with a number, use this listing.

The places in this list are also listed in the Index.

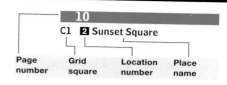

2

B3 **1** Chyandour Cl
2 Hellesvean
3 Hellesvean Cl
4 Parc-an-Stamps
5 Crows-an-Eglos
6 Parc-an-Forth
7 Penbeagle Terr
8 Penbeagle Cres
9 Corva Rd
10 Priors Cl
11 Corva Cl
12 Porthia Rd
13 Carnstabba Rd
14 Alan Harvey Cl
15 Jubilee Ct
16 Tinners Way
17 Penbeagle Cl

10

C2 **1** Gwel-an-mor
2 Turnpike Hill
3 Shop Hill
4 Old Smithy Cl
5 Mount View Terr
6 Henfor Mews
7 St Levan Rd
8 St Levan Cl
9 Treworvenneth Dr
10 Forreglos Dr
11 Churchway
12 Henfor Cl
13 Henfor Terr

11

B2 **1** North Orchard Ct
2 Queen's Way
3 Retallack Gdns
4 Primrose La
5 Trevelyan Way
6 Orchard Way
7 Manor Farm Cl
8 Meadow View
9 Primrose Cl
10 Trevelyan Cl

13

B3 **1** Lynwood Cotts
2 Prevenna Rd
3 Gwelenys Rd
4 Parkryn Rd

5 Foxes La
6 Marcwheal
7 Dumbarton Terr
8 Southview Terr
9 Duck St
10 Commercial Rd
11 Quay St
12 North Cliff
13 Fore St
14 North St
15 Cherry Gdn St
16 Virgin Pl
17 Brook St
18 South Cliff
19 Grenfell St
20 Mill La
21 Chapel St
22 Wharf The
23 Portland Pl
24 Gurnick St
25 Raginnis Hill
26 St Clements Terr
27 Saltponds

14

A1 **1** Ayr Ct
2 Tregarthen
3 Southfields Pl
4 Windsor Terr
5 Bullans Terr
6 Trerice Rd
7 Carnellis Rd
8 Nanjivey Pl
9 Nanjivey Terr
10 Bostennack Pl
11 Bostennack Terr
12 Pearce's La
13 Middle Stennack Cotts
14 Stennack Gdns
15 Sandows La
16 Rosewall Cotts
17 Rosewall Terr
18 Fern Glen
19 Little-in-sight
B1 **1** St Andrew's St
2 Redfern Ct
3 Street-an-Pol
4 Tregenna Pl
5 Gabriel St
6 Bedford Pl

7 Wesley Pl
8 Windsor Hill
9 Drillfield La
10 Alma Terr
11 Trenwith Terr
12 North Terr
13 Umfulla Pl
14 Trenwith Pl
15 Dove St
16 Tregenna Hill
17 Street-an-Garrow
18 Skidden Hill
19 Fern Lee Terr
20 Sea View Terr
21 Albert Pl
22 Padnover Terr
23 Porthminster Terr
24 Petes Pl
25 Carrack Widden
26 Albert Terr
27 Harlequins
28 Rosemorran
29 Talland Ct
30 Stones Ct
B2 **1** St Nicholas Ct
2 Sail Loft Flats
3 Rope Wlk The
4 Island Rd
5 Penameyne Ct
6 Porthmeor Rd
7 Back Road E
8 Island Sq
9 Fish St
10 Bethesda Pl
11 Victoria Rd
12 Victoria Pl
13 Barnaloft
14 Piazza
15 North Pl
16 St Peters St
17 Back La
18 Church Pl
19 Chy-an-Chy
20 Baileys La
21 Porthmeor Sq
22 Bunkers Hill
23 Rose La
24 Love La
25 Digey The
26 Virgin St
27 Meadow Flats

28 Godrevy Terr
29 Barnoon Terr
30 Academy Terr
31 Market Strand
32 Lifeboat Hill
33 Market Pl
34 Bowling Gn
35 Bowling Green Terr
36 Carrack Dhu Est
37 Carrack Dhu
38 Bellair Terr
39 Mount Pleasant
40 Richmond Pl
41 Trewyn Flats
42 Back St
43 Atlantic Terr
44 Clodgy View
45 West Pl
46 Galleries The
47 Meadow The
48 Crusoe Flats
49 Digey Flats
50 Porthmeor Studios
51 Porthmeor Ct
52 Mount Zion
53 Wills La

22

C3 **1** Roscadghill Parc
2 Heabrook Parc
3 Nicholas Parc
4 Mythyon Ct
5 Hea Cotts
6 Haig Pl
7 Poltair Terr
8 Brookward Terr
9 Holly Terr
10 Carmen Sq
11 Wesley St
12 Sylverton Pl
13 Jamaica Terr
14 Jamaica Pl
15 Pleasant Pl
16 Nevada Pl
17 Melbourne Terr

23

A1 **1** Greenbank
2 Hawkins Ct
3 Trevean Gdns
4 Alverton Terr